HAWTHORNE'S
LOST
NOTEBOOK
1835–1841

HAWTHORNE'S LOST NOTEBOOK 1835–1841

Facsimile from
The Pierpont Morgan Library

Transcript and Preface by Barbara S. Mouffe

Introduction by Hyatt H. Waggoner

Foreword by Charles Ryskamp

The Pennsylvania State University Press
University Park and London

Library of Congress Cataloging in Publication Data

Hawthorne, Nathaniel, 1804–1864.
  Hawthorne's lost notebook, 1835–1841.

  Includes bibliography.
  1. Hawthorne, Nathaniel, 1804–1864—Manuscripts—
Facsimiles. I. Mouffe, Barbara S. II. Title.
PS1865.A1 1978   813'.3   78-50772
ISBN 0-271-00549-1

Designed by Glenn Ruby

Frontispiece:
Oil Portrait of Nathaniel Hawthorne by Charles Osgood, 1840
Courtesy of the Essex Institute, Salem, Massachusetts

Contents

Foreword

In March 1977, The Pierpont Morgan Library was able to add to its collections of all the known American Notebooks of Nathaniel Hawthorne the missing earliest Notebook, which he kept in Salem from 1835 to 1841. It was purchased by the Library through Goodspeed's Book Shop of Boston with funds provided by one of the Trustees of the Library, Mrs. Charles W. Engelhard. We are all deeply grateful for her kindness and her generosity. Her gift has made it possible for scholars to study and for everyone to read in the present volume the first major addition to the canon of Hawthorne's works in many decades.

In his Introduction, Professor Hyatt H. Waggoner writes that "in a number of ways the Notebook here presented may seem to the student of Hawthorne as man and writer the most important of all the Notebooks." The rest of the Notebooks, with the exception of an Italian Notebook of 1858 and two fragments of leaves from an English Notebook (in the Huntington Library), are in the Morgan Library: four volumes in all of American Notebooks, seven English Notebooks, and five French and Italian Notebooks. They are here with the two volumes of a journal which Hawthorne kept jointly with his wife, the manuscripts of *The Blithedale Romance* and *Tanglewood Tales,* the two pages (title page and contents) which are all that remain of his most famous work, *The Scarlet Letter,* and manuscripts of several of his best-known stories, portions of other novels or romances, letters, notes, etc. Altogether they form by far the most comprehensive collection of Hawthorne's manuscripts in existence.

The finding of Hawthorne's earliest Notebook has been one of the most exciting pieces of news in recent years concerning American literary history. In her Preface, Barbara Mouffe tells a fascinating story of the discovery and identification of the manuscript. It seems scarcely credible that it should have been finally identified on Hawthorn Avenue in Boulder, Colorado.

I should like to give special thanks to Professor Hyatt H. Waggoner, Mr. John M. Pickering of The Pennsylvania State University Press,

Mr. Gordon T. Banks of Goodspeed's Book Shop, and Mr. Herbert Cahoon and Mr. Charles Passela of the staff of the Morgan Library.

Charles Ryskamp
Director, The Pierpont Morgan Library

Preface

"A letter written a century or more ago, but which has never yet been unsealed"—Nathaniel Hawthorne, Manuscript Notebook, 1836–37[1]

Discovery and Identification

"In the cabinet of the Essex Historical Society, old portraits. . ."[2] I came upon this passage one day as I was attempting to decipher the handwriting in a little manuscript notebook which had belonged to my family for several generations.

The notebook I had in hand was small (4¾ by 7½ inches), bound in brown marbled cardboard covers with what appeared to be black leather on its spine and corners. The notebook was composed of 43 unpaginated leaves, all written on both recto and verso in black ink, the handwriting tiny and difficult to read, with ink smudges here and there throughout, and an occasional inked-out phrase or line. The book had originally contained 44 leaves, but the second leaf had been neatly cut out, and what apparently was a fragment of that page had been pasted back by its left edge onto the blank top portion of the third leaf, in such a way that it could be lifted up to reveal writing on its back. A later count disclosed that the notebook contained approximately 21,800 words, averaging 253 words per page. There was no name in it to signify its author or original owner.

The notebook had been kept for many years in our antique cabinet which had been inherited from my maternal grandparents, and which a fine arts appraiser had termed a Tudor Court Cupboard. None of us ever had an inkling that this cupboard was fated to take on a mystique similar to that of James Boswell's Ebony Cabinet (in which some of his own missing manuscripts were discovered generations after his death)!

My grandfather John Lillie, an American living in England, was editor of the London edition of *Harper's* magazine from 1880 to 1884.[3]

---

[1]References to "Manuscript Notebook" are to the one reproduced in the present volume. The dates show the period of composition, since Hawthorne did not date all his entries.
[2]Manuscript Notebook, 1837.
[3]Frank L. Mott, *A History of American Magazines,* vol. 2, p. 399. Complete bibliographical information for all references is in the Bibliography at the end of the Preface.

In September 1906, he and his wife, Amy (Reynolds) Lillie, purchased Ivy Hall, a house overlooking the river Thames in Richmond, Surrey. In order to furnish the house, Mr. Lillie frequented antique sales and auctions in London, and it was at one of these that he purchased the Tudor Court Cupboard, which is an early-seventeenth-century carved oak cabinet. It is about five feet tall, with two doors that swing out. Inside it are several shelves.

When the Lillies returned to America, the cupboard was among the treasures they selected to bring with them. Through the years between 1920 and 1953, households broke up, but the Tudor Court Cupboard remained in the family.

My grandmother Amy (Reynolds) Lillie had a bachelor brother, Walter Hamilton Reynolds, who died in Boston in 1944. He had had a sentimental devotion to his mother, Harriet Reynolds, who died leaving him an orphan when he was eighteen. (His father had died when he was two months old.) The attachment Walter had felt toward his mother compelled him to keep all her private papers, letters, diaries, and every scrap of written material belonging to her that he could find, and he preserved them for the remainder of his life. Could this notebook have been among those albums, diaries, and letters?

When my mother inherited the Tudor Court Cupboard, it became the repository for all such material, which came to be known in the family as the Archives. The cupboard and its Archives remained in her house in Dedham, Massachusetts, for many years, until her death.

Among her Uncle Walter's varied interests had been the tracing of his family history, which he recorded in typewritten genealogies of several family branches. In 1962 I discovered the genealogies among his other papers in the cupboard and became fascinated with pursuing them further. This interest led to my recent study of the history of Salem, Massachusetts, in order that I might learn about the birthplace of William James Reynolds, my great grandfather.

At the time I found the genealogies, I either overlooked the little manuscript notebook, or if I did look at it, I rapidly put it back in the Cupboard, finding the writing rather illegible, as had other family members, no doubt. So there it remained for fourteen more years.

After my mother's death in 1976, everything in her house was divided among my three sisters and myself, my twin sister receiving the Tudor Court Cupboard. I particularly wanted to take home its contents, the Archives, as I was the only one of us with both the time and interest in our family history to make use of them. I remember saying to my sisters, "Anything of value I unearth will of course belong to the four of us equally." We all laughed at this remark, especially as the appraiser had just valued the contents of the cupboard at the grand sum of twenty dollars!

Consequently, these family papers were shipped off to my home on Hawthorn Avenue in Boulder, Colorado, in two small trunks, which I found lying on my study floor when I reached home. There they remained for several weeks gathering dust. I finally decided something had to be done with them, so I started sorting through the contents, putting things in piles on the floor according to their probable ancestral origin.

Several times I picked up the little notebook, but as I could not easily read the writing, I returned it to one of the trunks, not knowing to which family branch it belonged. When at last I came to the bottom of the second trunk, there it still lay. So I decided to devote some time in earnest to discovering what it was.

The notebook was filled with tiny, scrawly writing on all the pages except the insides of the front and back covers. It appeared to consist of numerous entries. The space between each entry was marked by a row of horizontal dashes. Some of the entries had an X in ink across them or in the left margin beside them, and there were also penciled brackets beside some of them. Here and there I picked out a word or two, but it was only when I read the words "In the cabinet of the Essex Historical Society. . ." that anything in the notebook had meaning for me, for I immediately realized that this meant Essex County, and thus Salem, Massachusetts.

"At last," I thought, "I know whose this was; it belonged to my great grandfather, William James Reynolds, who was born in Salem in 1814!" This conclusion seemed to be corroborated by the dates that appeared here and there in the notebook, 1835 to 1841. The last date came on the back of the first leaf, showing that the author ran out of pages, so filled both sides of the blank front leaf last.

For the time being I put the notebook on the Reynolds pile of Archives, and turned to other matters. But inevitably I came back to it, my curiosity being aroused concerning my great grandfather. My great uncle Walter had saved some letters written by his father, W. J. Reynolds, so I looked at them in order to make a comparison of the handwriting. How amazed I was to find that my great grandfather's writing was altogether different from that in the notebook! His was large and bold, not tiny and hurried-looking. I was quite mystified by this, but then thought it might have been his wife's writing—wrong again!

The only thing to do, I decided, was to try to read the notebook and attempt to determine by the contents whose it was. I flipped through it at random, stopping here and there, endeavoring to decipher some of the entries. One entry for 1838 began, "In the old burial-ground, Charter St. a slate grave-stone, carved round the borders, to the memory of 'Col. John Hathorne, Esq.' who died in 1717. This was the witch-judge." Having just read Sidney Perley's three-volume *His-*

tory of Salem, Massachusetts, I knew that this entry referred to an ancestor of Nathaniel Hawthorne's who was involved with the Salem witch trials of 1692.

Reading more of the notebook I began to realize that the entries comprised three categories: descriptions of walks and excursions taken by the author, ideas and observations taken from books and magazines he had been reading, and, most intriguing of all, ideas for stories or articles he might write. Many of the entries had such ideas, starting with "A hint of a story—. . . ," or "An article might be made respecting . . . ," or ending with "Much may be made of this idea." Could this person have been a writer? I knew of none of my ancestors from Salem who were authors. Who might it have been? The only writer from Salem I had ever heard of was Nathaniel Hawthorne.

I was well aware that Nathaniel Hawthorne was one of America's foremost writers, but *The House of the Seven Gables* was the only one of his works I remembered having read, and that was years before, in school. I certainly had no knowledge that he had ever kept a journal or diary. Nevertheless, I opened my encyclopedia to "Nathaniel Hawthorne" and saw that he was born in 1804, finished college in 1825, and then spent a number of years living in Salem as a sort of recluse, wandering alone, making observations and gathering material for tales and sketches which were published in periodicals.[4] I found also that he kept notebooks which his widow later published as *Passages From the American Note-Books.* The dates in my notebook did seem to fit in with the encyclopedia information about Hawthorne. My excitement was beginning to intensify! Could I really be in possession of an original manuscript of the great writer Nathaniel Hawthorne? I tried not to be overly excited about this theory. Just because Hawthorne kept journals was no reason to think this notebook was one of them, I told myself. I had to find out more about Hawthorne before I should even consider such a theory.

The next day I went to my local public library and procured several books about Hawthorne. One had a facsimile of his handwriting taken from a manuscript he had written nearly twenty years later than the most recent date in my notebook. It appeared to be similar, but I hardly dared believe it was the same.

One of the books told of Hawthorne's American Notebooks: "The notebooks themselves were finally acquired by the Morgan Library. But one or more of the notebooks had been lost in the intervening years."[5] The last sentence seemed almost to jump out of the page at me!

---

[4]Manning Hawthorne, "Nathaniel Hawthorne." *Collier's Encyclopedia,* 1954, vol. 9, pp. 575–577.
[5]Malcolm Cowley, ed., *The Portable Hawthorne,* p. 546.

But it was when I started reading excerpts from the actual published passages that I really became excited. Some of them followed word for word what was written in my notebook, but further perusal showed me that many of them were not verbatim. Often a word or phrase was changed in the published version; sometimes a whole sentence of the manuscript was deleted. I wondered why, if this really was Nathaniel Hawthorne's notebook, some of the passages were different from the published ones, and why anyone would have presumed to have changed or improved upon Hawthorne's writing.

I procured from the library the complete *Passages From the American Note-Books.* Comparing these to my notebook, I soon found that not only did Mrs. Hawthorne change words and phrases, delete many parts, and reorder the sequence of the entries, she also neglected to publish a number of entire passages.

By this time I was virtually certain that I had Hawthorne's original manuscript of his earliest journal. How could I prove this, and how would I proceed when I had proven it? My first inclination was to verify that the handwriting was Hawthorne's. The library contained several books with facsimiles of his writing, so I showed these to a professional Questioned Document Examiner, a handwriting expert. She studied both the facsimiles and the manuscript for several hours at my home. I paced the floor while awaiting her verdict, and at last she emerged from my study saying jubilantly, "You've got Nathaniel Hawthorne's writing here, no question about it!"

Later, as the impact of my discovery penetrated more deeply, I was almost overcome by the knowledge that I alone in the whole world knew that in 1836 Hawthorne wrote in his notebook, "In this dismal *and squalid* chamber FAME was won"!

By now I had become completely absorbed in Nathaniel Hawthorne and was determined to read as many books as I could find about him. The more I read the more I began to realize that this "lost notebook" contained valuable and significant information about Hawthorne and his writing that no scholar had as yet seen, and which would give insight that might well be of great help in the continuing study of this important American writer.

Transcription and Comparison with Published Notebooks

How could I make this "lost notebook" available to the literary world? I decided first to transcribe the manuscript in order to find out just what it contained. For the next several weeks I proceeded to copy it all, cover to cover, word for word, down to the last punctuation mark, often having difficulty with the tiny writing, but finding it easier as I became familiar with it. I was eventually able to decipher all but approximately four or five words of the manuscript, with the exception of a few words that had been inked out. In my transcription I noted each spot where a new manuscript page had begun, using my own numbering system, as Hawthorne had not numbered his pages.

For the purpose of comparing my transcription with the published version, I procured the Ohio State University Centenary Edition of the works of Nathaniel Hawthorne, *The American Notebooks*, Volume VIII, edited by Claude M. Simpson. This I used as my textbook, noting beside each printed entry the page number in the manuscript where it appeared. Then beside each entry in my transcription I wrote the page number from the published version. If an entry had not been published, I wrote "unpublished" beside it in my transcription. I was thus able not only to see to what extent the sequential order of entries had been changed when published, but also to determine the number of entire entries that had been omitted.

Next, I carefully went through my whole transcription, using Simpson's published text, as well as the original manuscript notebook, noting all the changes (in words, phrases, omissions, additions, punctuation) that Mrs. Hawthorne had made when she edited this first American Notebook. Each of these changes I inserted in my transcription directly over the line where the change occurred. This enabled me to see the extent of Mrs. Hawthorne's alterations of the original manuscript.

(It should be noted that the contents of my manuscript notebook comprised all the material that the Ohio State Centenary Edition labeled "Notebook I" and "Notebook III." The Centenary Edition editor, having had no access to the original manuscript, erroneously assumed that Hawthorne took up a new notebook on his return from his Maine visit during the summer of 1837,[6] whereas in reality he resumed writing in this notebook. This assumption may have been derived from letters written by Sophia Hawthorne to her publisher, James T. Fields, in October 1865, while she was in the process of transcribing the notebooks for publication. She says, "I have copied from the first note-book of 1835 and 1836," and "I suddenly have come to the end of 1836 and now comes the Maine journal of 1837."[7] The editor evidently interpreted her statements to mean that Hawthorne not only came to the end of 1836, but to the end of the notebook as well.)

Next I proceeded to list all the complete entries in the manuscript which were not published—a total of 71 out of approximately 330

[6]*Nathaniel Hawthorne, The American Notebooks.* Claude M. Simpson, ed., p. 701.
[7]Randall Stewart, "Editing Hawthorne's Notebooks—Selections from Mrs. Hawthorne's letters to Mr. & Mrs. Fields, 1864–1868," pp. 302–303.

entries, or about 21½ per cent. I thus ascertained how much of the manuscript is totally "new." Then for the purpose of my analysis I continued by listing words Hawthorne used that Mrs. Hawthorne omitted, words she changed, phrases she omitted, phrases she changed, words Hawthorne misspelled that Mrs. Hawthorne corrected, and entries Mrs. Hawthorne combined. I also listed words I was unable to decipher, and words Mrs. Hawthorne mistranscribed.

Now that I had all this information, what could I do with it, how could I make it available to the public, and how could I verify the manuscript's authenticity from a scholarly standpoint? My twin sister, Mary, Mrs. Irving O. Anderson, lives in Rhode Island and is acquainted with Hyatt H. Waggoner, Professor of English at Brown University in Providence, Hawthorne scholar, and author of *Hawthorne: A Critical Study.* She consulted with him as to how to proceed. He suggested that I bring him the notebook, so my husband and I traveled east with it, and he verified that indeed it was one of Hawthorne's missing notebooks. Professor Waggoner studied my transcription and advised me that it should be published. He agreed to be the scholar to announce the discovery to the public at the Hawthorne conference sponsored by the Nathaniel Hawthorne Society to be held a few months later at Bowdoin College in Brunswick, Maine.

Search for Origin, Acquisition

Professor Waggoner felt that it would be useful to try to ascertain how the manuscript came into my family's possession. He said it would be of interest if I could prove that the notebook had been given to us by Nathaniel Hawthorne or his heirs, or failing that, if I could determine that at least there had been a connection between Hawthorne and a member of my family.

Consequently I launched into a period of concentrated inquiry, studying as many biographical sources on Hawthorne as I could find. I also undertook further research into my own family background, finding a possible connection between Hawthorne and a member of my family. (A peripheral discovery has been that I share common ancestors with both Hawthorne and his wife, Sophia Peabody Hawthorne.) However, I have been unable to prove, *other than by its very existence,* that the notebook was given to my family by Hawthorne or his heirs. Nowhere in my reading did I find any clues as to the disposition of the missing notebook, only that it is "now lost," or is "no longer extant."

My investigation has shown that the literary world of Boston in Hawthorne's era was rather close-knit; there seemed to be friendly associations among booksellers, publishers, printers, and authors of the period. Boston was a much smaller community in those days, with a population of about 24,000 in 1800, increasing to 100,000 by 1850.[8] Booksellers and publishers tended to be concentrated in one or two neighborhoods of the city, and seem therefore to have been mutually acquainted.

One man in this literary world happened to be my maternal great grandfather, William James Reynolds, who was born in Salem ten years after Nathaniel Hawthorne. Reynolds moved to Roxbury from Salem in about 1835 and became a bookseller and publisher. His obituary in the *Norfolk County Journal* of Roxbury, January 21, 1865, says: "By good judgment in the purchase of copyrights, he soon became prosperous, and removed his business to Boston, where it was very extensive." Another obituary mentions his being a member of the Massachusetts Legislature of 1863. The *Boston Almanac* for 1844 lists him as "William J. Reynolds, Publisher, 20 Cornhill." By 1849 the *Boston Directory* shows he had moved his business to 24 Cornhill.

I have found that Mr. Reynolds had connections with several people in the literary world of Boston who also had connections with Nathaniel Hawthorne, and who therefore might have formed the link I was looking for. These people were Samuel G. Goodrich, William D. Ticknor, John P. Jewett, and George C. Rand. I have also determined that Reynolds was in at least two places at the same time as Hawthorne (one in 1853, one in 1862), suggesting again a possible acquaintance between the two.

From as early as 1853 until at least 1863 William James Reynolds was associated with George C. Rand, the printer of the first edition of *Uncle Tom's Cabin*.[9] In 1853 Rand and Reynolds published a series of twenty books, "The Cabinet Library," all written by another Roxbury resident, Samuel G. Goodrich, who used the pseudonym Peter Parley.[10] This association of Reynolds with Goodrich points to Reynolds's possible acquaintance with Nathaniel Hawthorne, for it was Goodrich who had published Hawthorne's work all through the 1830s in his Christmas giftbook, *The Token*. In 1836 Goodrich arranged for Hawthorne to edit *The American Magazine of Useful and Entertaining Knowledge*, and to write Goodrich's *Peter Parley's Universal History*.[11] In 1837 Goodrich arranged the publication of Hawthorne's *Twice-Told Tales*.[12]

---

[8]Andrew Hepburn, *Biography of a City—Boston*, p. 140.
[9]Hellmut Lehmann-Haupt, *The Book in America*, p. 119.
[10]Samuel G. Goodrich, *Recollections of a Lifetime*, vol. II, p. 542.
[11]Randall Stewart, *Nathaniel Hawthorne, A Biography*, p. 32; Goodrich, *Recollections*, vol. II, p. 544.
[12]Stewart, *Nathaniel Hawthorne*, p. 33.

Another associate of Hawthorne's with whom my great grandfather was acquainted was William D. Ticknor, partner in the firm Ticknor & Fields, Hawthorne's publishers. A letter written by Ticknor tells of Reynolds having been one of the passengers on the ship *Niagara*, which carried the Hawthornes and Ticknor to England in 1853. Ticknor was accompanying Hawthorne to help establish him as American Consul at Liverpool, and he was also using the journey as an opportunity to purchase books in Europe. Evidently Reynolds was on a European book-buying trip as well, for Ticknor writes in another letter of there being "a large number of American booksellers here this summer," and of being with Reynolds and other booksellers in Paris later that summer. It is entirely possible that Reynolds became acquainted with Hawthorne on board the *Niagara*, through their mutual friend Ticknor. There were 150 passengers and Ticknor mentions only four that he knew besides the Hawthornes and Reynolds.[13]

Reynolds was not only with Ticknor and Hawthorne in 1853, but I have also established that they all stayed at Willard's Hotel in Washington, D.C., for three days at the end of March and beginning of April 1862. Hawthorne and Ticknor had gone to Washington to obtain a clearer view of the progress of the Civil War, and they went close to the scenes of action, as well as attending a meeting with President Lincoln. In *Hawthorne And His Publisher,* Caroline Ticknor says, "The various excursions ended with a trip to Manassas, and the rainy days which prevented their doing any sight-seeing were agreeably spent at Willard's Hotel, which was, at that moment, the genuine center of Washington and the Union interests" (p. 279).

Reynolds was in Washington on business and was there only three days, staying at Willard's Hotel. He went to Alexandria, Virginia, on April 2. Hawthorne and Ticknor also visited Alexandria at some time before Hawthorne left Washington (on approximately April 6) for home,[14] but I have not determined whether they were at Alexandria on the same day as Reynolds, only that all three were at Willard's Hotel.

I have a letter addressed to Reynolds at Willard's Hotel from his wife, Harriet, dated April 2, 1862, which says:

> Mr. Charles Ellis expected to reach Washington on Tuesday [April 1, 1862]. I suppose you have seen him. Mr. E. P. Tilestone [her mother's first cousin], Mr. Ticknor and Mr. Bryant went to Washington and were anxious to get passes for Fortress Monroe. Gov. Andrew appointed them Commissioners and they were received as guests and shown all that they desired to see.[15]

[13]Caroline Ticknor, *Hawthorne And His Publisher,* pp. 51–75.
[14]Horatio Bridge, *Personal Recollections of Nathaniel Hawthorne,* p. 174.
[15]Ticknor, *Hawthorne And His Publisher,* p. 278, says, ". . . the friends [Hawthorne and Ticknor] were appointed upon a special committee to visit the Fortress officially. . . . "

This letter does not mention Hawthorne but it does suggest the possibility that he and my great grandfather were acquainted through their mutual friendship with W. D. Ticknor.

Another connection Reynolds had with the literary world of Boston was with John P. Jewett, bookseller and publisher. Jewett was the same age as Reynolds, in 1836 lived at 43 Federal Street in Salem and was a partner with John M. Ives in Ives and Jewett, booksellers, at 193 Essex Street, Salem, according to the town directory. The *Salem Directory* for 1842 shows that Jewett then lived with Henry Whipple (also a bookseller) at 2 Andover Street. It also shows that John Dike, Nathaniel Hawthorne's uncle by marriage (he married Hawthorne's aunt, Priscilla Manning), lived next door to Jewett at number 4 Andover Street.[16]

The *Salem Tax Valuations* lists for 1831–1834 show that the Reynolds family lived at Gedney Court, between Summer and High streets, which was only a few blocks from both Andover Street and Federal Street (where Jewett had lived before his Andover Street residency). The population of Salem in 1835 was only about 13,000, so Reynolds and Jewett might easily have become acquainted while they were both living in Salem, and Jewett might also have known Hawthorne through John Dike.

By 1847 Jewett had moved his business to 23 Cornhill in Boston, according to the city directory. As we have seen, Reynolds in 1847 had his business at 20 Cornhill, moving it to 24 Cornhill in 1849, both addresses being in close proximity to Jewett's.

Jewett was the publisher of Harriet Beecher Stowe's *Uncle Tom's Cabin.* One of my sisters has the 1853 one-volume illustrated edition of this book, and inscribed on its flyleaf is the following:

> W. J. Reynolds, with the Respects of
> the Publishers, Boston   April 19, 1853

The Hawthornes were also acquainted with Harriet Beecher Stowe. Annie Adams Fields, the wife of James T. Fields (Ticknor's partner and Hawthorne's publisher and friend), wrote: "In July, 1860, we returned to America, Mrs. Harriet Beecher Stowe and her family, and Mr. Hawthorne and his wife and children accompanying us."[17] It is conceivable that because William James Reynolds knew John P. Jewett (Mrs. Stowe's publisher) and George C. Rand (the printer), he may also have become acquainted with Mrs. Stowe and through her, with Hawthorne. Reynolds's acquaintance with Ticknor could also have led to an acquaintance with James T. Fields, and thus with Hawthorne. It does indeed

---

[16]Vernon Loggins, *The Hawthornes,* p. 256.
[17]*James T. Fields—Biographical Notes And Personal Sketches,* p. 83.

appear as if W. J. Reynolds moved in some of the same circles as Hawthorne, and could easily have known him.

W. D. Ticknor died in April 1864, which rules out his having given Reynolds the notebook, because Nathaniel Hawthorne still had it at his own death in May 1864, several weeks after Ticknor's. William J. Reynolds died in January 1865, eight months after Hawthorne. Neither Hawthorne nor Mrs. Hawthorne could have given Reynolds the notebook because Mrs. Hawthorne was still copying from it in October 1865, after the deaths of both her husband and Reynolds. Her *Passages From the American Note-Books* appeared in twelve installments in *The Atlantic Monthly,* starting in January 1866. What happened to the notebook in the next few years is not known.

It is logical to suppose that the notebook was no longer in the possession of Hawthorne's daughter Rose by 1876, because her husband, George Parsons Lathrop, in his *A Study of Hawthorne* (pp. 62–63), erroneously perpetuated the error of the editor of *Passages* (Sophia Hawthorne) by quoting "(Salem, Union Street)" following the passage "In this dismal chamber FAME was won." Had Lathrop seen the manuscript he would have known that Hawthorne not only followed "dismal" with "and squalid," but he added no location for the chamber, which appears only in Mrs. Hawthorne's printed version.

Also, when Lathrop in 1883 wrote the introductory notes to the Riverside Edition of *Passages* (Works, 1883, IX, 10), he guessed incorrectly as to the identity of "B_____," a mistake he would not have made had he seen the manuscript, which clearly shows "B_____" to be Bridge in an 1835 entry. The Centenary Edition of *The American Notebooks* declares, ". . . one must assume that he had not inspected the notebook itself."[18]

It is also logical to assume that the manuscript was no longer in the possession of Julian Hawthorne, the other surviving heir, by 1884. In his *Nathaniel Hawthorne And His Wife* (Cambridge, 1884), Julian quotes some unpublished entries from Hawthorne's later notebooks, but none from the first one.

Julian inherited his father's American notebook manuscripts from his mother after she died in 1871, and later, "a considerable quantity of great Hawthorne material—inscribed copies, letters, and manuscripts—was peddled by Julian Hawthorne during his various financial crises."[19] A collector, Stephen H. Wakeman, came into the possession of Hawthorne's notebooks in 1903; in 1909 he sold them, through George S.

---

[18]Centenary Ed., p. 564, note to 8.27.
[19]Randall Stewart, *The American Notebooks by Nathaniel Hawthorne,* p. vii; Matthew J. Bruccoli, "Hawthorne as a Collector's Item, 1885–1924," in *Hawthorne Centenary Essays,* Roy Harvey Pearce, ed., vol. IV, p. 478.

Hellman, to J. Pierpont Morgan. But the manuscript of this first note-book was not included in that sale. If Julian had had the notebook, surely he would have sold it with the others.

On September 4, 1867, Mrs. James T. Fields wrote in her diary while at her summer home at Manchester-by-the-Sea, Massachusetts:

> Wednesday. A quiet day—some reading and writing and much dally-ing out of doors although the weather was not clear. Jamie came down late. He had a very busy day in town. Mrs. Hawthorne has brought him 14 closely written volumes of her husband's journal—all so fine as to be difficult to read, from that reason and for no other, for there are no corrections. Such marvellous accuracy of observation and such strange records of interesting people and places were perhaps never before made. There are also piles on piles of romances begun but never finished—chapters here and there of exquisite beauty but nothing complete.[20]

Assuming that this notebook of the years 1835 to 1841 was among the manuscript journals Mrs. Hawthorne brought to Mr. Fields at that time, this diary entry is the latest mention of its existence I have found, some two years after Mrs. Hawthorne's allusion to it in her letter of October 1865, written when she was transcribing it.[21] Everything I have found written about the notebook since then has described it as "lost" or "missing."

It is clearly possible that Mrs. Hawthorne could have given it to the Fieldses as a memento in September 1867, "as indeed, after their return from abroad, the Hawthornes were more closely associated with the Fields than with any other family."[22] She was known to have given away as favors souvenirs of Hawthorne's writing.[23]

If in fact Mrs. Hawthorne did not at that time make a gift of the notebook to the Fieldses, it could have been separated, inadvertently, from the mass of unpublished material she brought Fields on Septem-ber 4, and not have been returned to her before she left for Germany in October 1868. This would not have been the only time Fields misplaced a manuscript she had given or sent him, for in January 1868 Mrs. Hawthorne wrote to Fields concerning her transcription of the manuscript of "Twenty Days with Julian and Little Bunny." She said, "I am especially distressed that the Copy is lost somewhere in your House. . . . "[24]

James T. Fields died in 1881, leaving to his widow, Annie, manu-scripts of several authors. George S. Hellman, the agent through whom

---

[20]Annie Adams Fields, *Journal of Literary Events and Glimpses of Interesting People.*
[21]Stewart, "Editing Hawthorne's Notebooks," p. 302.
[22]Stewart, *Nathaniel Hawthorne, A Biography,* p. 217.
[23]Centenary Ed., vol. VIII, p. 687.
[24]Stewart, "Editing Hawthorne's Notebooks," p. 312.

J. Pierpont Morgan acquired Hawthorne's other manuscript notebooks, wrote, "Almost all of Hawthorne's manuscripts have, at one time or another, come to me."[25] But he did mention seeing the manuscript of Hawthorne's *The House of the Seven Gables,* as well as manuscripts of other authors, at the Boston home of Mrs. Fields. Could Hawthorne's manuscript notebook have been there as well? He wrote, "It was Mrs. Fields's intention (as it had been her husband's wish) that her treasures should go to Harvard University; but every now and then—when Christmas came around—she would part with a few manuscripts in order to swell the sum of her benefactions."[26]

Mrs. Fields died in 1915, leaving to Harvard University the manuscript of *The House of the Seven Gables,* as had been her husband's desire, but I have found no evidence suggesting that she was at that time in possession of Hawthorne's notebook.

All my investigation has led me to the conclusion that the missing notebook was among papers belonging to Annie Adams Fields. She may very well have been on friendly terms with my great grandmother, Harriet Reynolds, possibly having met her through William D. Ticknor. Both she and Harriet Reynolds were married to publishers and they were approximately the same age (Mrs. Fields was born in 1834, Mrs. Reynolds in 1833). They also happened to be fourth cousins, both being descended from Peter and Ann Boylston of Boston.[27] Mrs. Fields, in her diary for October 1865, writes that she "walked to Roxbury Sunday and heard a noble discourse from Dr. Putnam." The Reynoldses, who lived in Roxbury, were married by Dr. Putnam in 1861 and attended his church, so could have known the Fieldses in this way as well as through publishing and bookselling circles.

Though neither Harriet Reynolds nor other personal friends were mentioned in Annie Fields's diaries, the title she herself put on them, *Journal of Literary Events and Glimpses of Interesting People,* could easily explain that omission. Annie Fields wrote in her diaries almost exclusively about authors or wives of authors with whom she had personal contact.

Harriet Reynolds might well have been the recipient of this notebook from Annie Fields "when Christmas came around." Mrs. Fields felt bitterly hurt over the quarrel about money matters between Sophia Hawthorne and Mr. Fields, as is shown in her diary entry of Friday, August 7, 1868:

[25]George S. Hellman, *Lanes of Memory,* p. 30.
[26]Ibid., p. 29.
[27]Andrew N. Adams, *A Genealogical History of Henry Adams of Braintree, Mass. and his Descendants, 1632–1897,* pp. 394, 395, 401, 410, 429, 460.

> He [JTF] brought down strange news this afternoon! I know we do not
> live by chance nor do we arrange the circumstances of life but when a
> friend, to whom we have been devoted as we have been to Mrs. Haw-
> thorne, listens to Gail Hamilton and allows herself to be persuaded that
> we have treated her dishonestly, it seems as if wonders and pains were not
> to be prepared for in this world by the wildest achievements of imagina-
> tion . . . All this towards *us,* too, whom she has ever esteemed her best and
> truest. She clean forgets her husband's faith and her husband's wish. . .

Could these hurt feelings have been such that Mrs. Fields was willing to
part with a reminder of the quarrel, and to give the notebook to the
widow of her husband's fellow publisher?

Harriet Reynolds died on November 2, 1883. Her eighteen-year-
old son, Walter, may not have known what the little manuscript notebook was, but he seems certainly to have been the one who preserved it
with the rest of his mother's papers, and when he died it was placed in
the Tudor Court Cupboard, not to be discovered until more than one
hundred years after it was written. What mysterious workings of fate
caused it to pass undisturbed from generation to generation? The impact of this was brought to me in a startling way when I read one of
Hawthorne's story ideas, on page 37 of his manuscript notebook: "A
letter, written a century or more ago, but which has never yet been
unsealed."

Publication

Until now, the only version of this notebook has been the one which
was printed not from Hawthorne's manuscript, but from his widow's
edited transcription of the manuscript. Therefore the currently defini-
tive published version, The Centenary Edition, contains not only Sophia Hawthorne's editing of her husband's original, but the publisher's
editing of her transcription, making it twice removed from the original
manuscript. Recognizing, as did Randall Stewart, that "the American
Notebooks are a classic, a unique classic, in their own right,"[28] I feel it
is therefore most important that this notebook be published in as nearly
as possible its original form.

Nathaniel Hawthorne himself wrote, in "A Book of Autographs":

> And, in truth, the original manuscript has always something which print
> itself must inevitably lose. An erasure, even a blot, a casual irregularity of
> hand, and all such little imperfections of mechanical execution, bring us
> close to the writer, and perhaps convey some of those subtle intimations
> for which language has no shape.[29]

[28]"Editing the American Notebooks," p. 279.
[29]*The Works of Nathaniel Hawthorne,* vol. XII, pp. 88–89.

Bibliography

The Works of Nathaniel Hawthorne. With introductory notes by George Parsons Lathrop. Boston & New York: Houghton, Mifflin & Co. (Riverside Edition), 1883. 12 vols.

The Centenary Edition of the Works of Nathaniel Hawthorne. Columbus: Ohio State University Press, 1962–1977. Vol. VIII: *The American Notebooks.* Claude M. Simpson, ed. 1972.

Adams, Andrew N. *A Genealogical History of Henry Adams of Braintree, Mass. and his Descendants, 1632–1897.* Rutland, Vt., 1898.

Beebe, Maurice and Hardie, Jack. "Criticism of Nathaniel Hawthorne: A Selected Checklist." *Studies in the Novel,* vol. 2, no. 4 (Winter 1970), pp. 519–587.

Boston Almanac, 1844.

Boston Directory, 1847 and 1849.

Bridge, Horatio. *Personal Recollections of Nathaniel Hawthorne.* New York: Harper and Brothers Publishers, 1893.

Bruccoli, Matthew J. "Hawthorne as a Collector's Item, 1885–1924." In *Hawthorne Centenary Essays,* Roy Harvey Pearce, ed. Columbus: Ohio State University Press, 1964. Vol. IV, pp. 387–400; note p. 478.

Clark, C. E. Frazer, Jr. *Nathaniel Hawthorne: A Descriptive Bibliography.* Pittsburgh: University of Pittsburgh Press, 1978.

Cowley, Malcolm, ed. *The Portable Hawthorne.* New York: Viking Press, 1948.

Fields, Annie Adams. *James T. Fields—Biographical Notes and Personal Sketches.* Boston: Houghton, Mifflin & Co., 1882.

Fields, Annie Adams. *Journal of Literary Events And Glimpses of Interesting People.* Unpublished manuscript diaries at the Massachusetts Historical Society, Boston, 1863–c.1915.

Goodrich, Samuel G. *Recollections of a Lifetime.* New York and Auburn, N.Y.: Miller, Orton & Mulligan, 1856. 2 vols.

Hawthorne, Julian. *Nathaniel Hawthorne And His Wife.* Cambridge: James R. Osgood & Co., 1884. 2 vols.

Hawthorne, Manning. "Nathaniel Hawthorne." *Collier's Encyclopedia,* 1954, vol. 9, pp. 575–577.

Hawthorne, Nathaniel. Manuscript Notebook, 1835–1841.

Hawthorne, Sophia, ed. *Passages From the American Note-Books of Nathaniel Hawthorne.* Boston: Ticknor and Fields, 1868. 2 vols.

Hellman, George S. *Lanes of Memory.* New York: Alfred A. Knopf, 1927.

Hepburn, Andrew. *Biography of a City—Boston.* New York: Scholastic Book Services, 1966.

Jones, Buford. "Current Hawthorne Bibliography." *The Nathaniel Hawthorne Society Newsletter,* vol. I, no. II (Fall 1975), pp. 4–6; vol. II, no. 2 (Fall 1976), pp. 4–10; vol. III, no. 2 (Fall 1977), pp. 6–10.

Lathrop, George Parsons. *A Study of Hawthorne.* Boston: Houghton, Mifflin & Co., 1876.

Lehmann-Haupt, Hellmut. *The Book in America.* New York: R. R. Bowker Co., 1952.

Loggins, Vernon. *The Hawthornes. The Story of Seven Generations of an American Family.* New York: Columbia University Press, 1951.

Mott, Frank L. *A History of American Magazines.* New York and London: D. Appleton & Co., 1930. 2 vols.

Perley, Sidney. *The History of Salem, Massachusetts.* Salem, Mass.: Published by the Author. 1924, 1926, 1928. 3 vols.

Ricks, Beatrice. *Nathaniel Hawthorne: A Reference Bibliography, 1900–1971,* with selected 19th century materials. Boston: G. K. Hall, 1972.

Salem Directory, 1836, 1842.

Salem Tax Valuations, 1831–1834.

Stewart, Randall. *The American Notebooks By Nathaniel Hawthorne.* Based upon the Original Manuscripts in The Pierpont Morgan Library And Edited by Randall Stewart. New Haven: Yale University Press, 1932.

Stewart, Randall. "Editing the American Notebooks." *Essex Institute Historical Collections,* vol. 94 (July 1958), pp. 277–281.

Stewart, Randall. "Editing Hawthorne's Notebooks." Selections from Mrs. Hawthorne's letters to Mr. & Mrs. Fields, 1864–1868. *More Books.* The Bulletin of the Boston Public Library. Vol. XX (September 1945), pp. 299–315.

Stewart, Randall. *Nathaniel Hawthorne—A Biography.* New Haven: Yale University Press, 1948.

Ticknor, Caroline. *Hawthorne And His Publisher.* Boston & New York: Houghton, Mifflin & Co., 1913.

Waggoner, Hyatt H. *Hawthorne: A Critical Study.* Cambridge: Belknap Press of Harvard University Press, 1955; rev. ed. 1963.

Acknowledgments

I would like to thank the following for their assistance in bringing this project to completion:

My husband, Frank, and my sons, Frank, David, and Eric, for their forbearance and encouragement while I was spending every waking moment indulging myself in Nathaniel Hawthorne.

Hyatt H. Waggoner of Brown University for his authentication of the manuscript, his announcement of its discovery, his encouragement and help in this publication, and for his scholarly introduction to this volume.

Manning Hawthorne of Chapel Hill, North Carolina, for his gracious permission to publish my transcript of his great grandfather's manuscript.

Arlin Turner of Duke University, for his encouragement, and also his search at the Huntington Library among the Hawthorne collection for mention of my great grandfather, W. J. Reynolds.

Raymona Hull of Indiana, Pennsylvania, for her interest and her constructive suggestions as to my line of research, and her sharing of her knowledge of the Hawthornes after the death of Nathaniel.

W. S. Tryon of Rockport, Massachusetts, for his search for mention of W. J. Reynolds at Harvard University's Widener Library in its collection of *Boston Transcripts.*

John D. Cushing, Librarian of The Massachusetts Historical Society, for allowing me to search through Annie Adams Fields's manuscript diaries.

Ruth Nuzum of Boulder, Colorado, for her interest and moral support and for allowing me to make use of her extensive library of Hawthorne First Editions, many of which I was unable to obtain from local libraries.

John Graham of the University of Colorado, for his advice and encouragement, and for allowing me to sit in on his Hawthorne Seminar, at which I gained a much clearer insight into Nathaniel Hawthorne and his writing.

Herbert Cahoon, Curator of Autograph Manuscripts, and Francis S. Mason, Jr., Assistant Director, at The Pierpont Morgan Library, for their help in arranging this publication by The Pennsylvania State University Press.

Others who have been most supportive are Arthur Monke, Librarian of Bowdoin College; Marjorie Elder of Marion College; and William H. Bond, Director of Harvard University's Houghton Library. Irene Norton, Reference Librarian at the Essex Institute, Salem, Massachusetts, was extremely helpful in my research.

I would like to thank especially my three sisters, Betsy Crowder, Mary Anderson, and Ellen Tennant, for their constant and continuing encouragement, and for their allowing me complete freedom in the disposition of the notebook. Betsy made many useful suggestions; Mary and her husband, Andy, were instrumental in my meeting Hyatt H. Waggoner; and Ellen was most helpful in the preparation of my preface (even to the extent of going to Salem with me for research).

Last but not least, I wish I could thank Sophia Hawthorne for her help in deciphering Nathaniel Hawthorne's handwriting. Her *Passages From the American Note-Books of Nathaniel Hawthorne* was of major help to me, though even she occasionally misread some of his words!

Barbara S. Mouffe

Introduction

The publication of this Reader's Edition of the earliest Notebook Hawthorne is known to have kept gives us the first major addition to the canon of Hawthorne's writings since Randall Stewart's faithful version of the then extant American notebooks in 1931. Before Barbara Mouffe discovered and identified the manuscript early in 1976, we had known it only from the bowdlerized excerpts from it to be found in Mrs. Hawthorne's *Passages From the American Note-Books,* which was serialized in *The Atlantic Monthly* in 1866, two years after Hawthorne's death, and published in book form in 1868. The last known references to the Notebook itself are to be found in Mrs. Hawthorne's letters to her publisher while she was at work preparing it for the public. What happened to it after that no one knows, though Mrs. Mouffe has presented the available inconclusive evidence concerning how it may have come into the possession of one of her ancestors.

In 1909 the wealthy collector Stephen Wakeman sold five Hawthorne Notebooks to the even wealthier collector J. Pierpont Morgan, who later established The Pierpont Morgan Library, where all the extant American Notebooks kept by Hawthorne, including the newly discovered one, may now be found. Working from the five purchased by Morgan—numbers II, V, VI, VII, and VIII, according to the numbering system adopted by the late Claude Simpson in his Centenary Edition of the American notebooks—Randall Stewart gave us what Hawthorne had actually written in the five Notebooks. In 1972, when Stewart's edition had long been out of print, the Centenary Edition made the text of the Morgan Notebooks available to the public again, adding to them the originally published texts of the edited versions of the present Notebook, mistakenly assuming it was two Notebooks which were numbered I and III, and of another lost one, number IV according to the Centenary system, which Hawthorne's daughter Rose Hawthorne Lathrop had sold in 1895 and which had been printed in *The Atlantic* in 1896, after which the original was lost. This little Notebook, in which Hawthorne made a half dozen entries recording his experiences while working in Boston Custom House in 1839, is now the only one he is known to have kept which is still lost.

In a number of ways the Notebook here presented may seem to

the student of Hawthorne as man and writer the most important of all the Notebooks. Not only is it the earliest, it is the only Notebook written wholly in Salem before his marriage in 1842 to Sophia Peabody, thus giving us our best evidence of what his life must have been like, and how he felt, during the latter part of what have been called his "years of solitude." Unlike the other Notebook he used during the years this Notebook covers, which he devoted to detailed descriptions of his experiences during his trips to Maine and the Berkshires in the summers of 1837 and 1838, this one is not wholly outward-centered, though it does record in its longest entries what he saw and heard on solitary walks around Salem and on trips to Boston and elsewhere.

Another feature of the newly discovered Notebook which gives it unique importance is the fact that it contains more notes for stories and what Hawthorne often referred to loosely as "articles" than any of the other Notebooks. The only other Notebook to be compared with it in this respect is the much longer one he began to use for journalizing after this one had been filled up. Covering the years from 1841 to 1852, the later one contains some 105 such entries in its eighty-six leaves, compared with this Notebook's approximately 161 entries in its smaller forty-three leaves. Though Sophia included her edited versions of the majority of such entries in her *Passages,* the ones we have not known before because she decided for one reason or another to omit them are often very revealing indeed of the quality of Hawthorne's imagination and the kinds of subjects that preoccupied him during these years.

Though they were not the completely "solitary" years they have been called, and Hawthorne was not really the "recluse" he describes himself as being in this Notebook, they were lonely and not very happy ones, judging by what he wrote here. When he began the Notebook he had been out of college for a decade, reading, writing for the magazines and gift-book annuals anonymously or pseudonymously, and planning three volumes of collected tales for book publication—for the periodicals and annuals offered little reward in either money or fame—only to see all three projected works fail of publication. He had written and published *Fanshawe,* which he quickly recognized as unworthy and tried to destroy and never cared to acknowledge even to his wife. Though he had already published some of his very greatest tales, including "My Kinsman, Major Molineux," "Roger Malvin's Burial," and "Young Goodman Brown," he had failed to achieve either recognition or a livelihood as a writer. His prospects were dim and much of the time his spirits must have been low. We are likely to emerge from reading the Notebook straight through feeling that it is not really surprising that nearly all of the works that have impressed modern readers as his greatest had either been written before 1835–1841 or would be produced later. During the last years covered by the Notebook, Hawthorne appears to have written less and with generally diminished power.

About three-fourths of the contents of this Notebook may be found, often with alterations and omissions, in Sophia's *Passages,* which of course announced in its title that it would present not the Notebook itself but those portions of it the editor thought suitable for public reading. Sophia's editing standards were those of her time, not those of the modern scholarly editor, and many of the alterations in Hawthorne's text she made when she copied passages from it, or in some cases the editor or printer of her copy may have made, would have been made by any editor of her day.

The late Claude Simpson made a point, in his "Historical Commentary" in the Centenary Edition, of the fact that Sophia sought, and presumably valued, the advice of her publisher Fields as she edited, the implication being that the scholarly indignation expressed by Randall Stewart, prompted by his discovery of the significant differences between the text of Sophia's *Passages* and that of the manuscript notebooks he was the first scholar to examine, was unscholarly and unjustified. It certainly was excessive and, no doubt unconsciously, self-promoting. But there is no evidence concerning how much advice she received from Fields, and anyway it would have been difficult for him to advise her without having seen the notebook itself from which she was making a printer's copy. Since there is no reason to believe he saw the manuscript notebook before 1867, it is reasonable to assume that it was she who silently corrected Hawthorne's occasional misspellings and mental lapses, added subjects or verbs to his incomplete sentences, and sometimes improved, as she thought, his wording, generally with the effect of making it more "literary" and conventional. But differences of this sort between Hawthorne's text and the one presented in *Passages* are neither particularly surprising nor particularly revealing.

Her omissions—and they almost certainly were hers—are a different matter. In deciding what to omit, she would appear to have been guided, whether consciously or not, by three motives: her desire to make her book interesting reading for the growing number of Hawthorne's admirers, her concern to protect the privacy of individuals, particularly when the relations between Hawthorne and herself were involved, and her sense that it was her duty to her husband to present to the public only those aspects of Hawthorne that he himself would have wanted to reveal.

The deletions apparently prompted by her first motive, reader interest, were no great loss to the general reader, then or now. Mostly notes drawn from Hawthorne's reading, they often prompt us to wonder why Hawthorne thought them worth recording. Hawthorne's strong interest in the past would explain some of them, but the items that might be described as "curious lore" are harder to account for. "Salt butter, being kept all night in milk, will become fresh. . . . Mustard and cress-seeds will take root and grow in wet flannel." Some of the entries of this sort were probably written (they are not dated) while Hawthorne was editing the *American Magazine of Useful and Entertaining Knowledge* and were used there, but since similar trivia were recorded both prior to and following the six months of his editorship in 1836, they remain something of a problem for the student of Hawthorne trying to understand his mind, and boring for the general reader.

Sophia's omissions to protect the privacy of individuals are likely to seem more regrettable not just to the biographer but to the reader who is simply interested in Hawthorne's work and so in his life. Thus his good friend Bridge appears in her version of the Notebook only as "B," even though nothing that Hawthorne wrote could possibly have given offense to his friend. Thus too the nineteen quotations from her so-called Cuba Journal are all left out, forcing earlier biographers to speculate more than they would have had to about the when and how of the relationship that culminated in an at first secret engagement.

Surely the most striking of such omissions consists of only two words from a one-sentence entry Hawthorne penned when he saw the first notices of *Twice-Told Tales,* not only his first book after so many years of unsuccessful attempts to publish one but the first piece of writing to appear under his own name. Sophia's version, often quoted, reads "In this dismal chamber FAME was won," omitting the words "and squalid" that Hawthorne had added after "dismal." It seems probable that the deletion was prompted by a desire to protect the feelings of the Mannings, Hawthorne's mother's family, to whose home Mrs. Hawthorne had returned after the death of her husband when Hawthorne was only four, the home where Hawthorne had, when he wrote, lived most of his life as an adult in the famous third-floor chamber. The living Mannings would surely not appreciate having a room in their house described as "squalid," that is, in its common meaning, dirty, neglected, poor, mean.

But if the reason why Sophia felt she had to omit "squalid" seems clear enough, Hawthorne's writing it is more of a puzzle—until we recall a now uncommon metaphoric use of the word that Hawthorne, whose business was words, would have been familiar with from his reading. For several centuries before Hawthorne wrote it the word was frequently used to mean impure, morally polluted, morally shameful, much as we today make a metaphor out of dirt when we say "dirty joke." If this is the meaning Hawthorne had in mind, then the word is as subjectively used as "dismal." With both words, he would have been ascribing his emotions to the room where he felt those emotions: he had felt "dismal," depressed in this room, and he had felt guilty, ashamed. If this is what he meant, then he would of course not have wanted the public to read it, so that what was no doubt Sophia's effort to protect the feelings of the Mannings had the effect of protecting her husband too. The sentence as he wrote it would seem to offer confirmation for what several critics of Hawthorne have long suspected, that he suffered from unusually strong guilt feelings.

Sophia's third motive for deleting entries or portions of entries may be described negatively, as Randall Stewart did in his edition of the then extant American Notebooks, as Sophia's remolding Hawthorne to fit the ideal prescribed by her conventional, prudish, determinedly genteel Victorian tastes and ideas, or, more sympathetically, as loyally protecting for her dead husband the reserve which he himself had maintained throughout his life. Hawthorne had written his Notebooks for his own use only, or, in the Old Manse years, sometimes for his and Sophia's eyes. If Sophia believed that Hawthorne would not have chosen to make his every thought public, she was undoubtedly right. Though he often spoke of himself and his writing in his Prefaces, he was being quite accurate when he reminded his readers in "The Old Manse" that "So far as I am a man of really individual attributes, I veil my face; nor am I, nor have ever been, one of those supremely hospitable people, who serve up their own hearts, delicately fried, with brain-sauce, as a tidbit for their beloved public."

Two of the "individual attributes" that Hawthorne chose not to exhibit to the public in his published writing become clear in this Notebook in passages Sophia chose to delete, as Hawthorne himself no doubt would have if he had aimed at publication, since he had no desire either to bare his heart or to offend public taste. He had a normal interest in, and could write without either prurience or euphemism about sex, and he could observe without registering shock or passing moral judgment such improprieties as public drunkenness; and his imagination was frequently drawn to subjects that involved cruelty, guilt and punishment, and suffering, decay, and death. Both in his public life and in his published writing, Hawthorne observed the Victorian proprieties and tried hard to avoid whatever might be considered morbid, lightening or moralizing it when it appeared, but in the Notebooks he felt no such constraint.

The contemporary reader is likely to smile at Sophia's proprieties and be drawn to Hawthorne when he reads such deleted passages as the one in the entry dated "June 22d" (1835) and beginning "A ride to Boston, in the afternoon" in which Hawthorne notes that he takes pleasure in seeing the shapes of girls' legs revealed by the wind, even though the girls themselves do not strike him as "pretty," or the later deleted passage in the same entry in which he observes with no suggestion of shock or condemnation a drunken couple supporting each other in Charlestown, with the woman succeeding in behaving with what he describes as "propriety" even though she was too drunk to walk straight.

Our response to the deletions of "morbid" entries, chiefly ideas for stories that never were written, is likely to be rather different. If they seemed morbid to Sophia, they seem so to us too. Why, we wonder, would Hawthorne think of writing a history of the "modes of punishment" practiced through the ages, or imagine a man sealing a woman he has loved in a cavern, driving her insane with his cruel treatment, and feeling "a loathing delight in his cruelty"? What traits of imagination prompted him to set down the following idea for a story that was never written: "To contrive some very great calamity for unsuspecting people, and then, while it is rolling inevitably onward, calmly to watch the result"?

The suggestiveness of this and many other hitherto unknown passages has made it seem desirable to The Pierpont Morgan Library and The Pennsylvania State University Press to make this Reader's Edition of the Notebook available for general reading by all those with a special interest in Hawthorne before a fully scholarly edition can be prepared. With the complete text before him, every reader can make his own interpretation of what is revealed by a reading of what Hawthorne actually wrote and all that he wrote.

My own impressions of what the Notebook reveals about Hawthorne are offered as just that, impressions, useful insofar as they prompt readers to check them against their own. The writer who emerges from this Notebook seems to me very clearly not a "thinker," not concerned with the current of thought in his day or with conceptual, philosophic, or theological problems of any sort. His interests are in the past, in the "real world" outside himself, in the workings of the human psyche under stress, the "deeper psychology," and in curious facts, especially if they suggested what he once called "the moral picturesque." Somewhat less clearly, the Notebook seems to suggest that Hawthorne suffered, as I have already said, from guilt feelings; that he felt alienated, an "outsider," who was aware of and did not like his alienation and longed for intimate ties to others; and that he exhibited a strong tendency toward voyeurism, toward seeing without being seen. None of these traits strikes me as wholly surprising, but no other Notebook seems to me to reveal them so clearly.

Henry James remarked long ago on the tourist-observer quality of the European Notebooks when Sophia's version of them was published, on the lack of interesting thought in them and their concentration instead on descriptions of the sights any tourist might see, pretty much as any tourist would see them. But after all, Hawthorne *was* a "tourist" in Europe, while this Notebook was written by a Salemite in Salem, yet still, in its diary entries describing walks and trips, foreshadows the quality James complained about in the later Notebooks. And when he was not describing the "real world" in and around his native town, or recording ideas for stories and sketches, he set down historical or curious facts gleaned from his reading. There is no suggestion here that he was at all concerned with the abstract ideas that his contemporary Emerson was occupied with during the years covered by this Notebook. But of course he was an artist, not a thinker.

That he suffered from very strong guilt feelings has been inferred by Freudian critics and others from his published writings, which when they are most impressive deal so often and with such subtle depth of penetration with situations involving secret guilt and the resulting isolation or alienation. The Notebook offers strong confirmation of the inference. If the interpretation I have offered of why he described his third floor chamber as not only "dismal" but also "squalid" is correct, then in that entry he is confessing to himself his feelings not only of depression but of guilt. In any case, it would be guilt feelings that would cause his mind to turn so often to the kinds of situations described in what I have called his "morbid" entries. No wonder he could write with such power about guilt: he knew what it felt like from his own experience.

As for what I have called his alienation, his diary entries in the Notebook suggest that he felt nearly as much an outsider in Salem as he would later in Rome. In his descriptions of his solitary walks in and around Salem, there is never a suggestion of meeting friends or neighbors. He had his friends of course, chiefly the several he had made in college, but even when he took a trip to Ipswich with his good friend Bridge and seems to have been in good spirits, Bridge is mentioned only as his companion on the ride. What did Bridge say or do? What did the two talk about? Except for the initial mention of Bridge and a later "we," Hawthorne might well have been alone.

Finally, the tendency toward voyeurism, which is so clear in the ironic self-portraiture as Coverdale in *The Blithedale Romance,* is suggested here in a number of entries. The trait is connected of course with Hawthorne's alienation, as is clear enough in the entry beginning "To stand, in a dark, cheerless evening, and look down into the cellar kitchen of a tavern," in which Hawthorne pictures himself at once as an outsider and as an unseen observer. That Hawthorne was aware of this trait in himself is clear in "Sights from a Steeple," in which he describes what he can see while remaining unseen and wishes that he might be a "spiritualized Paul Pry," able to look into the hearts of those he sees, while presumably still remaining unseen himself.

Apart from his lack of interest in abstract thought, which he apparently never regretted even during the Old Manse years when contact with the advanced thought of the time led him to write several of his finest sketches, these traits—guilt feeling, alienation, voyeurism—seemed to Hawthorne personal liabilities that he wanted very much to grow beyond or overcome. To some extent he seems to have succeeded during the first blissful years of his marriage, as the contents and tone of the Concord entries in the Notebook covering 1841–1852 suggest, but the traits never wholly left him and tended to return as the years went by.

But since he was a writer gifted with both creative imagination and acute self-knowledge, he was often able to turn his personal liabilities into artistic assets, creating from the "day-dreams and night dreams" that troubled him so sorely as a man some of the greatest fiction in our literature.

Hyatt H. Waggoner

A Note on the Text of the Transcript

The printed transcript presents as nearly as possible a clear text of what Hawthorne actually wrote in this earliest known Notebook. His occasional misspellings, for instance, are reproduced without comment, and mental lapses are noted only when it seemed possible that the reader of the printed transcript might be misled if he did not examine closely the corresponding passage in the facsimile. Similarly, no attempt has been made to regularize Hawthorne's inconsistent hyphenation. Likewise, both the photographic facsimile and the printed transcript present Hawthorne's entries in the order in which the reader would see them if he held the Notebook itself in his hand. Thus the first two entries, dated 1840 and July 29th, 1841, were written after Hawthorne had filled the rest of the Notebook and had turned back to use the front and back of the first leaf, which he originally had left blank.

Departures from the aim of presenting an exact transcription have been kept to a minimum. Roman type within brackets indicates conjectured or undecipherable words, except for the bracketed "other book" on page 78, where the brackets are Hawthorne's own. Italic type within brackets indicates editorial comment or explanation. These interruptions of the text are infrequent enough so that the reader may easily check the problems in the facsimile. The reader will also note in the facsimile that Hawthorne sometimes added information or made corrections interlinearly. This material appears in the transcript preceded and followed by slant lines (/). In addition, several paragraphs of the facsimile appear with a large X through them or with an X in the margin; the X has not been reproduced in the transcript. Finally, although page numbers do not appear in Hawthorne's Notebook, bracketed page numbers as well as dates of the entries do appear at the top of each page of the transcript as an aid to the reader.

Not easily checked is Hawthorne's punctuation, which is sometimes too indistinct or hastily penned to be deciphered with any real certainty. In such cases, the transcript presents what Barbara Mouffe and I decided together was apparently Hawthorne's intention. It seemed undesirable to interrupt the text with editorial comment on every questionable comma. Hawthorne's habits when proofreading his published texts suggest how little he was concerned about such matters.

This Reader's Edition is designed to make available and easily read-able what Hawthorne wrote, not to explain or analyze it. The reader who so wishes may make his own comparisons between the text here available for the first time and the text to be found in Sophia Hawthorne's *Passages From the American Note-Books,* reprinted in the Centenary Edition of the American Notebooks.

H.H.W.

HAWTHORNE'S
LOST
NOTEBOOK
1835–1841

Facsimile from The Pierpont Morgan Library
Transcript by Barbara S. Mouffe

Words—so innocent and powerless as they are, as standing in a
dictionary, how potent for good and evil they become, in the
hands of one who knows how to combine them!
—*Nathaniel Hawthorne*
American Notebook, 1848

1840   A contemplation

A man, unknown, conscious of a secret
crime, puts up a note in church, desiring the prayers of the congregation
for one so tempted.

—

Some most secret thing, valued
and honored between lovers,
~~to be hung up in~~
public places, and be made the object of remark — remarks,
jeers, laughter,

—

To make a story out of a scarecrow,
giving it queer attributes. From different points of view, it should appear to change — being an old man
or woman, a scarecrow, a gentleman, the
Old Nick &c.

— —

A ground sparrow's nest, in the
slope of a bank, brought to view
by mowing the grass, but still sheltered and comfortably hidden by a blackberry vine trailing over it. At first, four
brown speckled eggs — then two little bare young ones, which, on the
slightest noise, lift their heads, and open
wide mouths for food — immediately

1840

A man, unknown, conscious of /ˆtemptation to/ secret crime, puts up a note in church, desiring the prayers of the congregation for one so tempted.

Some most secret thing, valued and honored between lovers [*words in parentheses inked out*] to be hung up in a public place, and be made the subject of remark by the city—remarks, sneers, laughter.

To make a story out of a scarecrow—giving it queer attributes. From different points of view, it should appear to change sex, being an old man or woman, a gunner, a farmer, the Old Nick &c.

A ground sparrows nest, in the slope of a bank, brought to view by mowing the grass, but still sheltered and comfortably hidden by a blackberry vine trailing over it. At first, four brown speckled eggs— then two little bare young ones, which, on the slightest noise, lift their heads, and open wide mouth for food—immediately dropping their heads, after a loud gobble. The action looks as if they were making a most earnest, agonized petition. In another egg, as in a coffin, I could discern the quiet, deathlike head of the little bird. The whole thing had something awful and mysterious in it. – June 29th. 1841

—

A coroner's inquest on a murdered man – the gathering of the jury to be described, and the characters of the members; some with secret guilt upon their souls.

—

To represent a man as spending life and the intensest labor, in the accomplishment of some mechanical trifle – as in making a miniature coach to be drawn by fleas, or a dinner service to be put into a cherry-stone.

—

A coffin to be made of the gallows, and of all emblems of evil – or as a remedy; guns canopy &c &c &c

—

The love of posterity is a consequence of the necessity of Death. If a man were sure of living forever, he would not care about his offspring.

dropping their heads, after a broad gape. The action looks as if they were making a most-earnest, agonized petition. In another egg, as in a coffin, I could discern the quiet, deathlike head of the little bird. The whole thing had something awful and mysterious in it— June 29th. 1841

A coroner's inquest on a murdered man—the gathering of the jury to be described, and the characters of the members; some with secret guilt upon their souls.

To represent a man as spending life and the intensest labor, in the accomplishment of some mechanical trifle—as in making a miniature coach to be drawn by fleas, or a dinner service to be put into a cherry-stone.

A bonfire to be made of the gallows and of all symbols of evil, such as bands, gun carriages, &c &c &c

The love of prosperity is a consequence of the necessity of Death. If a man were sure of living forever, he would not care about his offspring

A phantom of the old Royal Governors, or some such shadowy pageant, on the night of the evac-uation of Boston by the British.

May 28th. 1835. The Circus.— A dancing horse, keeping excellent time to the music, with all four feet. Mr. Deakin says, that two horses, who had learned to dance, dropt down dead during their performance. The physical exertion seems very moderate; it must be the mental labor that kills them.— The Clown in his dress of motley, ma-king fun of everything.— Mr. Merryman.— the most antique character I suppose now existing; just the same, probably, that he used to be five hundred years ago; and perhaps playing off many of the identical jokes that all those pre-ceding generations have roared at.— A fellow who kept up several balls in the air at once; and also several knives,— this, too, is a feat of great antiquity, practised by the Saxon gleemen.— Ex-cellent horsemanship,— one rider with a boy on his shoulders; another man got into a sack, and after riding a few minutes, behold a wo-man emerged from the sack.— Feats of strength, by a young fellow of no great bulk, but very solid muscle; lifting a table and a boy on it, with his teeth; sustaining an anvil on his breast, where one another man smote with a sledge-hammer; laying out horizontally with his feet against a stout pole, high up in the air, and letting a boy walk out on his back.— The fellow seemed awkward in deportment, and made a very quick and bashful bow, of his head, by way of bow to the spectators.— A small white dog; of divers accomplishments. Vaulting and tumbling— one fellow three fourteen somersets in succession;

[*FRAGMENT (pasted by left edge on page)*]
A phantom of the old Royal Governors, or some such shadowy
pageant, on the night of the evacuation of Boston by the British.

[*VERSO OF FRAGMENT*]
. . . think, but not be sure whether [they] dreamed or knew it, that the
[first husband] hard come from his tomb, and [*"come" through "and"
crossed out in ink*] [*one line inked out totally*]

May 28th. 1835.
The Circus— A dancing horse, keeping excellent time to the
music, with all four feet. Mr Dakin says, that two horses, who had
learned to dance, dropt down dead during their performance. The
physical exertion seems very moderate; it must be the mental labor
that kills them— The Clown in his dress of motley, making fun of
everything— Mr. Merryman—the most antique character, I suppose,
now existing; just the same, probably, that he used to be five hundred
years ago; and perhaps playing-off many of the identical jokes that all
those successive generations have roared at.— A fellow who kept up
several balls in the air at once; and also several knives;—this, too, is a
feat of great antiquity, practised by the Saxon gleemen.— Excellent
horsemanship,—one rider with a boy on his shoulders; another man
got into a sack, and after riding a few minutes, behold a woman
emerged from the sack— Feats of strength, by a young fellow of no
great bulk, but very solid muscle; lifting a table and a boy on it, with
his teeth; sustaining an anvil on his breast, whereon another man
smote with a sledge-hammer; laying out horizontally, with his feet
against a stout pole, high up in the air, and letting a boy walk out on
his back. The fellow seemed awkward in deportment, and made a very
quick and bashful bob of his head, by way of bow to the spectators—
A small white dog, of divers accomplishments— Vaulting and
tumbling—one fellow threw fourteen somersets in succession.

June 15th. A walk down to the Juniper. The shore of the coves strewn with bunches of seaweed, driven in by recent winds. Eel-grass rolled and bundled up, and, entangled with it, large marine vegetables, of an olive color, with round, slender, snake-like stalks, four or five feet long, and a great leaf twice as long, and nearly two feet broad; these are the herbage of the deep-sea. Shoals of fishes, at a little distance from the shore, discernible by their fins out of water. Among the heaps of seaweed, there were sometimes small pieces of painted wood, bark, and other driftage. On the shore, with pebbles of granite, there were round or oval pieces of brick, which the waves had rolled about, till they resembled a natural mineral. Huge stones tossed about, in every variety of confusion, some shagged all over with sea-weed, others only partly covered, others bare. The old ten-gun battery, at the outer angle of the Juniper, very verdant, and besprinkled with white-weed, clover-tops, butter-cups &c. The Juniper trees are very aged, and decayed, and moss-grown. The grass about the hospital is rank, being trodden, probably, by nobody but me. The representation of a vessel under sail, cut with a pen-knife, on the corner of the house. Returning by the almshouse, I stopt a good while to look at the pigs — a great herd — who seemed to be just finishing their supper. They surely are types of unmitigated sensuality;— some standing in the trough, in the midst of their own and others' victuals;— some thrusting their noses deep into the filth;— some rubbing their hinder-ends against a post;— some huddled together, between sleeping and waking, breathing hard;— all wallowing in each other's defilement;— a great boar swaggering about, with lewd actions;— a big-bellied sow, waddling along, with her huge paunch. Notwithstanding the unspeaka-

June 15th.

A walk down to the Juniper. The shore of the coves strewn with bunches of seaweed, driven in by recent winds.— Eel-grass, rolled and bundled up, and, entangled with it, large marine vegetables, of an olive color, with round, slender, snake-like stalks, four or five feet long, and a great leaf, twice as long, and nearly two feet broad; these are the herbage of the deep-sea. Shoals of fishes, at a little distance from the shore, discernible by their fins out of water. Among the heaps of sea weed, there were sometimes small pieces of painted wood, bark, and other driftage. On the shore, with pebbles of granite, there were round or oval pieces of brick, which the waves had rolled about, till they resembled a natural mineral. Huge stones tossed about, in every variety of confusion, some shagged all over with sea-weed, others only partly covered, others bare. The old ten-gun battery, at the outer angle of the Juniper, very verdant, and be-sprinkled with white-weed, clover-tops, butter-cups &c. The Juniper trees are very aged, and decayed, and moss-grown. The grass about the hospital is rank, being trodden, probably, by nobody but me. The representation of a vessel under sail, cut with a pen knife, on the corner of the house. Returning by the almshouse, I stopt a good while to look at the pigs—a great herd—who seemed to be just finishing their suppers. They surely are types of unmitigated sensuality;— some standing / ˄in/ the trough, in the midst of their own and others victuals;— some thrusting their noses deep into the filth;— some rubbing their hinder-ends against a post;— some huddled together, between sleeping and waking, breathing hard;— all wallowing in each other's defilement;—a great boar ~~going~~ /swaggering/ about, with lewd actions;—a big-bellied sow, waddling along, with her swag-paunch. Notwithstanding the unspeaka-

able filth with which these strange sensualists stuff all their food, they seem to
have a quick and delicate sense of smell.—
What strange and ridiculous looking animals! Swift himself could not have imagined anything nastier than they practise by
the mere impulse of natural genius. Yet
the Shakers keep their pigs very clean; and
with good advantage.

Sunday evening, going by the jail, the setting sun kindled up the windows, most cheerfully; as if there were a bright, comfortable light
within its darksome stone walls.

N.B. The legion of devils in the herd of swine—
what a queer scene it must have been!

July 18th. A walk over to North Salem,
in the decline of yesterday afternoon — beautiful weather, bright-sunny, with a western, or
north-western wind, just cool enough, and a
slight superfluity of heat. The verdure, both
of trees and grass, is now in its prime, the leaves
bright, elastic, all life. The grass fields are
plenteously bestrewn with white weed, large
spaces looking as white as a sheet by snow,
at a distance, yet with an indescribably warmer tinge than snow. Living white, intermixed with living green. The hills, and
hollows, beyond the Cold Spring, copiously
shaded principally with oaks of good growth,
and some walnut trees, with the rich
sun brightening in the midst of the open
spaces, and mellowing and fading into
the shade — and single trees, with their
cool spot of shade on the waste of sun — quite
a picture of beauty, gently picturesque.
The surface of the land is so varied, with
woodland amongst, that the eye cannot reach
far away, except now and then it is intercep-
ted, perhaps across the river, showing houses, or a meeting-house and surrounding village in upper Beverley. In one of the sun-

able filth with which these strange sensualists sauce all their food, they seem to have a quick and delicate sense of smell.— What strange and ridiculous looking animals! Swift himself could not have imagined anything nastier than they practise by the mere impulse of natural genius. Yet the Shakers keep their pigs very clean; and with good advantage.

Sunday evening, going by the Jail, the setting sun kindled up the windows, most cheerfully; as if there were a bright, comfortable light within its darksome stone wall.

N.B.— The legion of devils in the herd of swine—what a queer scene it must have been!

July [*sic*] 18th.

A walk over in North Salem, in the decline of yesterday afternoon—beautiful weather, bright-sunny, with a western, or north-western wind, just cool enough, and a slight superfluity of heat. The verdure, both of trees and grass, is now in its prime, the leaves bright, elastic, all life. The grass fields are plenteously bestrewn with white weed, large spaces looking as white as a sheet of snow, at a distance, yet with an indescribably warmer tinge than snow. Living white, intermixed with living green. The hills and hollows, beyond the Cold Spring, copiously shaded principally with oaks of good growth, and some walnut trees, with the rich sun brightening in the midst of the open spaces, and mellowing and fading into the shade—and single trees, with their cool spot of shade in the waste of sun—quite a picture of beauty, gently picturesque. The surface of the land is so varied, with woodland amongst, that the /ₐeye/ cannot reach far away, except now and then in vistas, perhaps across the river, showing houses, or a meeting-house and surrounding village in upper Beverley. In one of the sun-my bits of pasture, walled irregularly in with oak shudder. I saw a gray mare feeding, and as I drew near, a colt started up from amid the grass — a very small colt. He looked me in the face, and I tried to frighten him, so as to make him gallop; but he stretched his long legs, one after another, walked quietly to his mother, and began to suck — not without wetting his lips, not being very hungry. Then he scratched his head, alternately with each hind leg. He was a graceful little beast.

I bathed in the cove, overhung with maples and walnuts — the water cool and thrilling; and a distance it sparkled bright and blue in the breeze and sun. There were jelly fish swimming about, and others left to melt away on the shore. On the shore, sprouting amongst the sand and gravel, I found samphire, or rather saure, growing somewhat like asparagus; it is an excellent salad, at this season, self cut with an herb-like vivacity, and salty tender. I strolled slowly through the pastures, watching my long shadow, making grave, fantastic gestures in the sun. It's a pretty sight to see the sunshine bright being the extreme of a road, which shortly becomes deeply overshadowed by trees on both sides. At the cold spring — there little girls, from six to nine, were squatted on the stones in which the fountain is set, and paddling in the water; it was a pretty picture, and would have been prettier, if they had shown bare legs, instead of pantalettes; very large trees overhung them, and the sun was so nearly down, then a pleasant gloom among the spot somewhere, in contrast with these light and laughing little figures. On perceiving me, they rose up titteringly among themselves; it seemed that there was a sort of playful malice in those who

ny bits of pasture, walled irregularly in with oak shade, I saw a gray
mare feeding, and as I drew near, a colt started up from amid the
grass—a very small colt. He looked me in the face, and I tried to
frighten him, so as to make him gallop; but he stretched his long legs,
one after another, walked quietly to his mother, and began to suck—
just wetting his lips, not being very hungry. Then he scratched his
head, alternately with each hind leg. He was a graceful little beast.

I bathed in the cove, overhung with maples and walnuts—the
water cool and thrilling; at a distance it sparkled bright and blue in the
breeze and sun. There were jelly fish swimming about, and several left
to melt away on the shore. On the shore, sprouting amongst the sand
and gravel, I found samphire, or mutton sauce, growing somewhat like
asparagus; it is an excellent salad at this season, salt yet with an
herb-like vivacity, and eating tender. I strolled slowly through the
pastures, watching my long shadow, making grave, fantastic gestures in
the sun. It is a pretty sight to see the sunshine brightening the
entrance of a road, which shortly becomes deeply overshadowed by
trees on both sides. At the cold spring, three little girls, from six to
nine, were squatted on the stones in which the fountain is set, and
paddling in the water; it was a pretty picture, and would have been
prettier, if they had shown bare legs, instead of pantalettes. Very large
trees overhung them, and the sun was so nearly down, that a pleasant
gloom made the spot sombre, in contrast with these light and laughing
little figures. On perceiving me, they rose up tittering among them
selves; it seemed that there was a sort /ᴀof playful malice/ in those who

first saw me; for they let the other keep paddling, without warning her of my approach. I passed on, and heard them come chattering behind.

June 22d A ride to Boston, in the afternoon, with Mr. Procter; — a coolish day, with clouds, and intermitting sunshine, and a pretty fresh breeze. We stopped about an hour at the Maverick House, in the Spрумtuir branch of the city, at East Boston; — a stylish house, with doors painted in imitation of oak; a large bar, bells ringing; — the bar-keeper calls out, when a bell rings "No —; then a waiter replies, No — answered; and scampers up stairs, a ticket given by the hostler, on taking the horse and chaise, which is given to the bar-keeper when the chaise is wanted. The landlord few hundred drafted, with the whitest of linen, neatly plaited, and correct as a Lord Chamberlain. Waiters for Boston throng'd the house; some standing at the bar, watching the process of preparing tumblers of punch; others sitting at the windows of different parlors, from with allusion to different expense. The bill of fare for the day stuck up, beside the bar... fare for the day stuck up, beside the bar... Opposite this principal hotel, there was another called the Mechanics, which seemed to be equally thronged. I suspect that the company was about on a par in each; for at the Maverick House, though well dressed, they seemed to be merely tradesmen, gentlemen mostly young fellows — clerks in dry goods stores being the aristocracy of them. One gentleman, very fashionable in appearance, with a handsome cane, happened to stop here, and lift up his foot — and I noticed that the sole of his boot (which was exquisitely polished) was all worn out. I apprehend that some such minor deficiencies might

first saw me; for they let the other keep paddling, without warning her of my approach. I passed on, and heard them come chattering behind.

June 22ᵈ·

A ride to Boston, in the afternoon, with Mr. Procter;—a coolish day, with clouds, and intermitting sunshine, and a pretty fresh breeze. We stopped about an hour at the Maverick House, in the sprouting branch of the city, at East Boston;— a stylish house, with doors painted in imitation of oak; a large bar; bells ringing;— the bar-keeper calls out, when a bell rings 'No _____; then a waiter replies, No. _____ answered, and scampers up stairs. A ticket given by the hostler, on taking the horse and chaise, which is given to the bar-keeper when the chaise is wanted. The landlord fashionably dressed, with the whitest of linen, neatly plaited, and courteous as a Lord Chamberlain. Visitors from Boston thronging the house; some standing at the bar, watching the process of preparing tumblers of punch; others sitting at the windows of different parlors, some with faces flushed, puffing cigars. The bill of fare for the day stuck up beside the bar. Opposite this principal hotel, there was another called the Mechanics, which seemed to be equally thronged. I suspect that the company was about on a par in each; for at the Maverick House, though well dressed, they seemed to be merely Sunday gentlemen, mostly young fellows—clerks in dry-good stores being the aristocracy of them. One gentleman, very fashionable in appearance, with a handsome cane, happened to stop by me and lift up his foot—and I noticed that the sole of his boot (which was exquisitely polished) was all worn out. I apprehend that some such minor deficiencies might

have been detected in the general showiness of most of them. There were fails, too, but
not pretty ones; nor, on the whole, such good
imitations of gentility as their beaux. It was
pleasant, however, as they were there about the
island, to see the wind reveal their shapes,
their petticoats being few and thin, and short
withal, showing a good deal of the leg in
a stocking, and the entire shape of both
legs, with the mist of a flimsy gown floating about it. The belt about the waist has
an excellent effect, in contrast with the
freedom and looseness of the lower dress. —
There were as many people as are usually
collected at a muster, or similar occasions,
lounging about, without any apparent
employment; but it were absurd to make
a sketch of the mode of spending the Sabbath, by the majority of unmarried young
middling people in a great town. May
conscience smote me for doing the like, tho'
if I had been at home, I should only have
been reading. ██████ Most of the gentlemen had
spent cares, bosom-pins &c.

Crossing the ferry into Boston. we went
to the city tavern, where the bar room presented a Sabbath scene of repose — the people lounging in chairs, half asleep, smoking
cigars — generally with clean shirts and other
niceties of apparel, to mark the day. The
doors and blinds of an oyster and refreshment
shop, across the street, were closed; but I
saw people enter. There were two owls, in
a large cage, visible through a window
of the bar room; — speckled grey, with dark
blue eyes; — the queerest looking birds that
exist; — so solemn and wise; dozing away
the day, much like the rest of the people,

have been detected in the general showiness of most of them. There were girls, too, but not pretty ones; nor, on the whole, such good imitations of gentility as their beaus. It was pleasant, however, as they walked about the island, to see the wind reveal their shapes; their petticoats being few and thin, and short withal, showing a good deal of the leg in a stocking, and the entire shape of both legs, with the mist of a flimsy gown floating about it. The belt about their waist has an excellent effect in contrast with the freedom and looseness of the lower dress.— There was as many people as are usually collected at a muster, or similar occasions, lounging about, without any apparent enjoyment; but it may serve to make a sketch of the mode of spending the Sabbath, by the majority of unmarried young middling people in a great town. May conscience smote me for doing the like, tho' if I had been at home, I should only have /ˌbeen/ reading. [*words inked out*] Most of the gentlemen had smart canes, bosom-pins &c.

Crossing the ferry into Boston – we went to the city-tavern, where the bar-room presented a Sabbath scene of repose—stage people lounging in chairs, half asleep, smoking cigars—generally with clean shirts and other nicieties of apparel, to mark the day. The doors and blinds of an oyster and refreshment shop, across the street, were closed; but I saw people enter. There were two owls, in a back court, visible through a window of the bar-room;—speckled gray, with dark blue eyes;—the queerest looking birds that exist;— so solemn and wise; dozing away the day, much like the rest of the people, only that they looked weary. Their hooked beaks look like a hook-nose. I shall seem there—a stranger, here and there, poring over a newspaper. Many of the shop folks sitting in chairs on the pavement, in front of the doors.

We went to the top of the hill, where formed part of Gardiner Greene's estate, and which is now in the process of levelling—and partly already taken away, except the highest point, and a narrow path to ascend to it. It gives a admirable view of the city, being almost as high as the steeples and the dome of the State house, and overlooking the whole mass of brick-buildings and slated roofs, with glimpses of streets far below. It was really a pity to take it down. I noticed the stump of a very large elm, recently felled, no house in the city could have reared its roof so high as the roots of that tree, if indeed the church-spires did.

On our ride home, passing through Charlestown, we saw a man and woman, very respectably dressed, but so drunk that they could hardly walk. I did not notice the man particularly; but the woman had a queer air of decency and decorum, in the midst of her inebriety—thinking with all the little reason in her noddle, to behave with propriety—and succeeding to perfection; only she could not walk straight. But that they supported each other, both would probably have fallen in the road—certainly the lady. They appeared to be Irish.

Stages in abundance were passing the road; cumbrous with passengers, inside and out; also chaises, barouches &c. horsemen and footmen. We are a community of sabbath-breakers.

only that they looked wiser. Their hooked beaks look like a
hook-nose. A dull scene this—a stranger, here and there, poring over
a newspaper. Many of the stage folks sitting in chairs on the
pavement, in front of the doors.

We went to the top of the hill, where formed part of Gardiner
Greene's estate, and which is now in the process of levelling—and
pretty much taken away, except the highest point, and a narrow path
to ascend to it. It gives an admirable view of the city, being almost as
high as the steeples and the dome of the state house, and overlooking
the whole mass of brick-buildings and slated roofs, with glimpses of
streets far below. It was really a pity to take it down. I noticed the
stump of a very large elm, recently felled; no house in the city could
have reared its roof so high as the roots of that tree;— if indeed the
church-spires did.

On our ride home, passing through Charlestown, we saw a man
and woman, very respectably dressed, but so drunk that they could
hardly walk. I did not notice the man particularly; but the woman had
a queer air of decency and decorum in the midst of her inebriety—
striving with all the little reason in her muddle, to behave with
propriety—and succeeding to perfection; only she could not walk
straight. But that they supported each other, both would probably
have fallen in the road—certainly the lady. They appeared to be Irish.

Stages in abundance were passing the road, burthened with
passengers, inside and out; also chaises, barouches &c; horsemen and
footmen. We are a community of Sabbath-breakers.

Aug. 31st. A ride to Nahant, yesterday afternoon. Stopt at Rice's, and afterwards walked
down to the steam-boat wharf, to see the passengers land. It is queer how few good faces there
are in this world, comparatively to the ugly ones.
Scarcely a single passable one, in all this collection. Then to the Hotel; Barouches at the
doors, and gentlemen and ladies going to ride.
Gentlemen smoking round the piazza. Nothing
remarkable. Parkes, at Rice's, had one of
Bluxton's 'mind-drops' for a bosom-pin; it made
a very handsome one. Home after supper,
crossing the beach at about sunset. The tide
so far down, as just to give us a passage
the hard sand, between the sea and the loose
gravel. The sea calm and smooth, with
only the surf-wave whitening along the
beach. Several ladies and gentlemen on horseback, cantering and galloping, before and behind us. Occasionally, a chaise met us; or
a barouche, filled with ladies and children,
and one gentleman for all.

A hint of a story—some incident which
should bring on a general error; and the chief
actor is the incident to have something corresponding to the mischief which he caused.

Sept. 7th. A ride to Ipswich with Bridge. At the
tavern, an old fat man by Mayor and another old
fellow laughing and playing off jokes on each other; one being a rebbor in the others hat. One had
been a trumpeter to the Mayor's troop. Walking
about town, we knocked, for a whim, at the door
of a dark old house, and inquired if Miss Hannah
Lord lived there. A woman of about thirty came to
the door, with rather a confused smile, and a disorder about her bosom-coverings, as if she had
been disturbed while suckling her child. The
annoyance is surely great kindness. Entering the
burial-ground, where some indoors were building
a tomb, we found a good many old monuments, and
several tombs covered with slabs of red free-stone
or slate, and with arms sculptured on the slab,
or an inlaid circle of slate. On one slate grave-
stone, of the Rev. Matth. Rogers, there was a portrait of

Aug 31st.

A ride to Nahant, yesterday afternoon. Stopt at Rice's, and afterwards walked down to the steam-boat wharf, to see the passengers land. It is queer how few good faces there are in this world, comparatively to the ugly ones. Scarcely a single passable one, in all this collection. Then to the Hotel. Barouches at the doors, and gentlemen and ladies going to ride, gentlemen smoking round the piazza. Nothing remarkable. Barkeeper at Rices, had one of Benton's 'mint-drops' for a boosom-pin; it made a very handsome one. Home after supper, crossing the beach at about sunset. The tide so far-down, as just to give us a passage on the hard sand, between the sea and the loose gravel. The sea calm and smooth, with only the surf-wave whitening along the beach. Several ladies and gentlemen on horseback, cantering and galloping, before and behind us. Occasionally a chaise met us; or a barouche, filled with ladies and children, and one gentleman for all.

A hint of a story—some incident which should bring on a general war; and the chief actor in the incident to have something corresponding to the mischief which he caused.

Sept 7th

A ride to Ipswich with Bridge. At the tavern, an old fat country Major and another old fellow laughing and playing off jokes on each other; one tying a ribbon in the other's hat. One had been a trumpeter to the Major's troop. Walking about town, we knocked, for a whim, at the door of a dark old house, and inquired if Miss Hannah Lord lived there. A woman of about thirty came to the door, with rather a confused smile, and a disorder about her bosom-coverings, as if she had been disturbed while suckling her child. She answered us with great kindness. Entering the burial-ground, where some masons were building a tomb, we found a good many old monuments, and several tombs covered with slabs of red free-stone or slate, and with arms sculptured on the slab, or an inlaid circle of slate. On one slate gravestone, of the Rev. Nath[l] Rogers, there was a portrait of that worthy, about a third the size of life, carved in relief, with his cloak, hands, and wig, in excellent preservation; all the buttons of his waistcoat &c being done with great minuteness; the minister's pew on a level with his cheeks. It was an upright grave stone. Returning home, held a colloquy with a young girl about the right road, she had come out to head a pig, and was confused and also a little suspicious that we were making fun of her; yet answered us with a sly laugh and good nature; the pig all the time squealing for his dinner.

Disposed along the walls and suspended from the pillars of King's Chapel, (the original wooden structure) were coats of arms of the King, the successive Governors, and other distinguished men. In the pulpit, there was an hour-glass, on a large and elaborate brass stand.

St Augustin, at mass, changed all that were accursed to go out of the church. "Then a dead body arose, and went out of the church into the churchyard, with a white cloth on its head, and stood there till mass was done." It was a former lord of the manor, whom a curate had cursed, because he refused to pay his tithes. Augustin also commanded the dead curate to arise, and gave him a rod, "and then the dead body, kneeling, received penance thereby." He then ordered the lord to go again to his grave, which he did, and fell immediately to ashes. Augustin offered to pray for the curate that he might remain on earth to confirm men in their belief, but the latter refused, because he was in the place of rest.

A dealer in woman's black worsted stockings was so in love with the article, that after it was going out of fashion, he still continued to buy large quantities, and invested his whole property in them; so that, by the reduction of the price, he was totally ruined.

Dr. Caner was Rector of King's Chapel in 1776. He left Boston with the Royalists.

that worthy, about a third the size of life, carved in relief, with his cloak, bands, and wig, in excellent preservation; all the buttons of his waistcoat &c being done with great minuteness; the ministers nose on a level with his cheeks. It was an upright grave stone. Returning home, held a colloquy with a young girl about the right road; she had come out to feed a pig, and was confused, and also a little suspicious that we were making fun of her; yet answered us with a shy laugh and good nature; the pig all the time squealing for his dinner.

Displayed along the walls and suspended from the pillars of Kings Chapel, (the original wooden structure) were coats of arms of the King, the successive Governors, and other distinguished men. In the pulpit, there was an hour-glass, on a large and elaborate brass stand

St. Augustine, at mass, charged all that were accursed to go out of the church. "Then a dead body arose, and went out of the church into the churchyard, with a white cloth on its head, and stood there till mass was done." It was a former lord of the manor, whom a curate had cursed, because he refused to pay his tithes. Augustine also commanded the dead curate to arise, and gave him a rod, "and then the dead lord, kneeling, received penance thereby." He then ordered the lord to go again to his grave, which he did, and fell immediately to ashes. Augustine offered to pray for the curate that he might remain on earth to confirm men in their belief; but the latter refused, because he was in the place of rest.

A dealer in women's black worsted stockings was so in love with the article, that when it was going out of fashion, he still continued to buy large quantities, and invested his whole property in them; so that, by the reduction of the price, he was totally ruined.

Dr. Caner was Rector of King's Chapel in 1776. He left Boston with the Royalists.

The organ of King's Chapel was surmounted by a gilt crown in the centre, supported by a gilt mitre on each side. The governor's pew had Corinthian pillars and crimson damask tapestry. In 1727, it was lined with china; probably tiles.

The chimney of an old house: it might be fancied that witches, on their broomsticks, have often flown forth through it, on their midnight excursions.

A sketch to be given of a modern reformer—a type of the extreme doctrines on the subject of slaves, cold-water, and all that. He goes along the streets haranguing most eloquently, and is on the point of making many converts, when his labors are suddenly interrupted by the appearance of a keeper of a mad-house, whence he has escaped. Much may be made of this idea.

✳The change from a gay young girl to an old woman; the melancholy events, the effects, which have clustered around her character, and gradually imbued it with their influence; till she is a lover of sick chambers, taking pleasure in receiving dying breaths, and in laying out the dead; also, furnishes her mind full of funeral reminiscences, and acquaintances beneath the buried turf than above it.

The world is so sad and solemn, that things meant in jest are liable, by an overpowering influence, to become dreadful earnest; gaily dressed fantasies turning to ghostly and black-clad images of themselves.

A well concerted train of events to be thrown into confusion by some misplaced circumstance; unsuspected till the catastrophe, yet exerting its influence from beginning to end.

A story the here of which is to be represented as naturally incapable of deep care, and looking forward to the

The organ of King's Chapel was surmounted by a gilt crown in the centre, supported by a gilt mitre on each side. The governor's pew had Corinthian pillars and crimson damask tapestry. In 1727, it was lined with china; probably tiles.

The chimney of an old house: it might be fancied that witches, on their broomsticks, have often flown forth through it, on their midnight excursions—

A sketch to be given of a modern reformer—a type of the extreme doctrines on the subject of slaves, cold-water, and all that. He goes about the streets haranguing most eloquently, and is on the point of making many converts, when his labors are suddenly interrupted by the appearance of a keeper of a mad-house, whence he has escaped. Much may be made of this idea. [*The last sentence possibly added at a later time; handwriting is different, though probably Hawthorne's.*]

The change from a gay young girl to an old woman; the melancholy events, the effects of which have clustered in round her character, and gradually imbued it with their influence; till she is a lover of sick chambers, taking pleasure in receiving dying breaths, and in laying out the dead; also, having her mind full of funereal reminiscences, and more acquaintances beneath the burial turf than above it.

The world is so sad and solemn, that things meant in jest are liable, by an overpowering influence, to become dreadful earnest; gaily dressed fantasies turning to ghostly and black-clad images of themselves.

A well-concerted train of events to be thrown into confusion by some misplaced circumstance, unsuspected till the catastrophe, yet exerting its influence from beginning to end.

A story, the hero of which is to be represented as naturally capable of deep and strong passion, and looking forward to the time when he shall feel passionate love, which is to be the great event of his existence. But it so chances that he never falls in love, and at length gives up the expectation of so doing, and marries calmly, yet somewhat sadly, with sentiment merely of esteem for his bride. The lady might be one who had loved him early in life, but whom then, in his expectation of passionate love, he had scorned.

In the old burial ground at Edgartown, it is so long since the bodies have decayed, that the soul has returned to its original barrenness.

The scene of a story or sketch to be laid within the light of a street-lanthorn; the time, when the lamp is near going out; and the catastrophe to be simultaneous with the last flickering gleam.

The peculiar weariness and depression of spirits, which is felt after a day wasted in turning over a magazine or other light miscellany.— different from the state of the mind after severe study, because there has been no excitement, no difficulties to be overcome; but the spirits have evaporated insensibly.

To represent the process by which sober truth gradually strips off all the beautiful draperies with which imagination has enveloped a beloved object, till from an angel, she turns out to be a mere ordinary woman. This to be done without caricature — perhaps with a quiet humor interfused — but the prevailing impression being a sad one. The story might consist of the various alterations in the feelings of the absent lover, caused by successive events that display the true character of his mistress; and the catastrophe should take place at their meeting, when he finds himself equally disappointed in her person; or the whole spirit of the thing may here be reproduced.

time when he shall feel passionate love, which is to be the great event of his existence. But it so chances that he never falls in love, and at length gives up the expectation of so doing, and marries calmly, yet somewhat sadly, with sentiments merely of esteem for his bride. The lady might be one who had loved him early in life, but whom then, in his expectation of passionate love, he had scorned.

In the old burial ground at Edgartown, it is so long since the bodies have decayed, that the soil has returned to its original barrenness.

The scene of a story or sketch to be laid within the light of a street-lanthern; the time, when the lamp is near going out; and the catastrophe to be simultaneous with the last flickering gleam.

The peculiar weariness and depression of spirits, which is felt after a day wasted in turning over a magazine or other light miscellany.—different from the state of the mind, after severe study, because there has been no excitement, no difficulties to be overcome; but the spirits have evaporated insensibly.

To represent the process by which sober truth gradually strips off all the beautiful draperies with which imagination has enveloped a beloved object, till from an angel she turns out to be a mere ordinary woman. This to be done without caricature—perhaps with a quiet humor interfused—but the prevailing impression being a sad one. The story might consist of the various alterations in the feelings of the absent lover, caused by successive events that display the true character of his mistress; and the catastrophe should take place at their meeting, when he finds himself equally disappointed in her person; or the whole spirit of the thing may here be re-produced.

A person, even before middle age, may become a rusty and faded concern among the people with whom he has grown up from childhood; but by emigrating to a new place, he appears fresh, with the effect of youth, which may be communicated from the impressions of others to his own feelings.

In an old house, a mysterious knocking might be heard, on the wall, where had formerly been an old doorway, now bricked up.

Last evening, from the opposite shore of the North river, a view of the trees, mirrored in the water, which was as smooth as glass, with no perceptible tide or agitation, except a slight swell and reflux on the sand; although the shadow of the moon danced in it. The picture of the town perfect in the water—towers of churches, houses, with here and there a light gleaming near the shore above, and more faintly glimmering under water—all perfect, but somewhat more hazy and indistinct than the reality. There were many clouds already flitting about the sky,—and the picture of each could be traced in the water—the ghost of what was itself unsubstantial. The rattling of wheels heard long and far through the town. Voices of people talking on the other side of the river; the tones being so distinguishable, in all their variations, that it seemed as if what they said might be understood; but it was not so.

Two persons might be bitter enemies through life, and mutually cause the ruin of one another. Finally, meeting at the funeral of a grand-child, the offspring of a son and daughter married without their consent,—and who, as well as the child, had been the victims of their hatred—they might discover that the supposed ground of their quarrel was altogether a mistake—and then be made fully reconciled.

A person, even before middle age, may become a musty and faded concern among the people with whom he has grown up from childhood; but by migrating to a new place, he appears fresh, with the effect of youth; which may be communicated from the impressions of others to his own feelings.

In an old house a mysterious knocking might be heard, on the wall, where had formerly been an old doorway, now bricked up.

Last evening, from the opposite shore of the North river, a view of the town, mirrored in the water, which was as smooth as glass, with no perceptible tide or agitation, except a trifling swell and reflux on the sand; although the shadow of the moon danced in it. The picture of the town perfect in the water—towers of churches, houses, with here and there a light gleaming near the shore above, and more faintly glimmering under water—all perfect, but somewhat more hazy and indistinct than the reality. There were many clouds flitting about the sky;—and the picture of each could be traced in the water—the ghost of what was itself unsubstantial. The rattling of wheels heard long and far through the town. Voices of people talking on the other side of the river; the tones being so distinguishable, in all their variations, that it seemed as if what /ʌwas/ there said might be understood; but it was not so.

Two persons might be bitter enemies through life, and mutually cause the ruin of one another, and of all that were dear to them. Finally, meeting at the funeral of a grandchild, the offspring of a son and daughter married without their consent,—and who, as well as the child, had been the victims of their hatred—they might discover that the supposed ground of the quarrel was altogether a mistake—and then be woefully reconciled.

To stand, in a dark, cheerless evening, and look down into the cellar kitchen of a tavern, through windows even with the ground;—the room ruddily illuminated, and girls plucking about fowls and dig faces;—the most striking part of the scene, the fire place and broad blazing fire, all a bed bright blaze and live coals, no apparent smoke; and before it two immoderately long spits, one over the other, the undermost sustaining several turkies, the upper & every smoking pigs &c placed as by their drippings to baste the turkies.

× It might be stated as the closing circumstance of a tale, that the body of one the characters had been petrified, and still existed in that state.

On the common, about dusk, after a salute from two field pieces, the smoke lay long and heavily on the ground, without much spreading beyond the original space over which it had gushed from the guns. It was about the height of a man. The evening clear, but with an autumnal chill.

A young man to win the love of a girl, without any serious intentions, and to find that, in that love which might have been the greatest blessing of his life, he had confused up a spirit of mischief, which pursued him through his whole career—and this without any revengeful intentions on the part of the deserted girl.

Two lovers, or other persons on the most private business, to appoint a meeting in what each supposed would be a place of the utmost solitude—and to find it thronged with people.

To contrive some very great calamity for unsuspecting people, and then, while it is rolling inevitably onward, calmly to watch the result. × + + +— + — + —— + +

Some of the oaks are now (Octr 17th 1835) a deep brown red & others are changed to a light green, which, at a little distance, especially in the sunshine, looks the green of early spring. In some trees, different masses of the foliage show each of these & hues. The

To stand, in a dark, cheerless evening, and look down into the cellar kitchen of a tavern, through windows even with the ground;— the room redly illuminated, and girls gliding about with ruddy faces;— the most striking part of the scene, the fire-place and broad-blazing fire, all a good bright blaze and live coals, no apparent smoke; and before it two immensely long spits, one over the other, the undermost sustaining several turkies, the upper as many sucking pigs, so placed as by their drippings to baste the turkies.

It might be stated, as the closing circumstance of a tale, that the body of one the characters had been petrified, and still existed in that state.

On the common, about dusk, after a salute from two field-pieces, the smoke lay long and heavily on the ground, without much spreading beyond the original space over which it had gushed from the guns. It was about the height of a man. The evening clear, but with an autumnal chill.

A young man to win the love of a girl, without any serious intentions, and to find that, in that love which might have been the greatest blessing of his life, he had conjured up a spirit of mischief, which pursued him throughout his whole career—and this without any revengeful intentions on the part of the deserted girl.

Two lovers, or other persons on the most private business, to appoint a meeting in what they supposed would be a place of the utmost solitude—and to find it thronged with people.

To contrive some very great calamity for unsuspecting people, and then, while it is rolling inevitably onward, calmly to watch the result.

Some of the oaks are now (Octr 17th, 1835) a deep brown red & others are changed to a light green, which, at a little distance, especially in the sunshine, looks the green of early spring. In some trees, different masses of the foliage show each of these hues. The

walnut trees, some of them, have a yet more delicate green. Others are of a bright yellow – a sunny
yellow.

+ Salt butter, being kept all a night in milk, will
be some fresh.

+ Mustard and cress-seeds will take root and
grow in wet flannel.

+ People who died of the plague were buried in a healthy hill; and nearly a hundred
years after, five persons, digging in that hill,
uncovered some linen. They immediately covered it again; — nevertheless they all sickened
of putrid fever, and three of the five died.

    Two persons, by mutual agreement, to make
their wills in each others' favour; then to wait
impatiently for one another's deaths, and both to
be informed of the desired event, at the same
time. Both, in most joyous sorrow, hasten to be
present at the funeral, and find themselves both
hoaxed.

    The story of a man cold and hard-hearted,
and acknowledging no brotherhood with mankind. At his death, there might try to dig him a
grave, but, at a little space beneath the ground,
strike upon a rock, as if the earth refused to
receive the unnatural son into her bosom. Then
they would put him into an old sepulchre, where
the corpses and coffins were all turned to dust,
and he would be alone. Then the body would
petrify; and he having died in some characteristic act and expression, he would seem,
through endless ages of death, to repel society
as in life; and none would be buried in
that tomb forever. But it must be a new
tomb; else the former bodies would have
petrified also.   X

walnut trees, some of them, have a yet more delicate green. Others are of a bright yellow—a sunny yellow.

Salt butter, being kept all in night in milk will become fresh.

Mustard and cress-seeds will take root and grow in wet flannel.

People who died of the plague were buried in a heathy hill; and nearly a hundred years after, five persons, digging in that hill, uncovered some linen. They immediately covered it again;—nevertheless they all sickened of putrid fever, and three of the five died.

Two persons, by mutual agreement, to make their wills in each other's favour; then to wait impatiently for one another's deaths, and both to be informed of the desired event, at the same time. Both, in most joyous sorrow, hasten to be present at the funeral, and find themselves both hoaxed.

The story of a man cold and hard-hearted, and acknowledging no brotherhood with mankind. At his death, they might try to dig him a grave, but, at a little space beneath the ground, strike upon a rock, as if the earth refused to receive her unnatural son into her bosom. Then they would put him into an old sepulchre, where the corpses and coffins were all turned to dust, and he would be alone. Then the body would petrify; and he having died in some characteristic act and expression, he would seem, through endless ages of death, to repel society as in life; and none would be buried in that tomb forever. But it must be a new tomb; else the former bodies would have petrified also.

Oct. 26th. 1835. Caleb Foote was married to Mary White last Wednesday. Yesterday, Mr. Brazer preaching on the comet, observed that not one, probably, of all who heard him, would witness its re-appearance. Mrs. Foote shed tears. Poor soul! She would be content to dwell in earthly love to all eternity.

———

A prostitute to be represented as returning, for a single evening, to the home or friends of her innocence — they being ignorant of her present infamy. She shows their domestic circle — becomes modest and maiden-like — a pure and innocent affection is sprouting between her and a young man, and thus time passes till the moment of departure arrives. Then, with a proud and generous feeling, that shows her noble, though ruined nature, she takes leave of them, hinting at the circumstances that must prevent their ever meeting again, bids farewell to the young man, and in him to all dreams of virtuous love, to which she has forfeited her title — and returns to her own and evil way, which had become like a fate upon her. It was as if the devil had let her go back for a little while; but she heard his voice summoning her back.

———

A sermon transformed to church-bells.

———

Some treasure or other thing, to be buried, and a tree planted right over the spot, so as to embrace it with its roots.

———

A fulminating powder — two parts saltpetre — two pea-ashes, two sulphur.

———

A tree, tall and venerable, to be said by tradition to have been the staff of some famous man, who happened to stick it in the ground, and it took root.

———

A fellow without money, having 170 miles to travel, pretends a chain of puddles to be his legs, and lay down to sleep in a field; the town apprehends and commits him to a jail in the town whither he desired to go.

Octr 26th. 1835.

Caleb Foote was married to Miss White last Wednesday.

Yesterday, Mr. Brazer preaching on the comet, observed that not one, probably, of all who heard him, would witness its re-appearance. Mrs. Foote shed tears. Poor soul! She would be content to dwell in earthly love to all eternity.

A prostitute to represented as returning, for a single evening, to the home or friends of her innocence—they being ignorant of her present infamy. She shares their domestic mirth—becomes modest and maiden-like—a pure and innocent affection is sprouting between her and a young man—and thus time passes till the moment of departure comes. Then, with a proud and generous feeling, that shows her noble, though ruined nature, she takes leave of them, hinting at the causes that must prevent their ever meeting again, bids farewell to the young man, and in him to all dreams of virtuous love, to which she has forfeited her title—and returns to her sin and misery, which had become like a fate upon her. It was as if the Devil had let her go back for a little while: but she heard his voice summoning her back.

Cannon transformed to church-bells.

Some treasure, or other thing, to be buried, and a tree planted right over the spot, so as to embrace it with its roots.

A fulminating powder—two parts saltpetre—two pearlashes, two sulphur.

A tree, tall and venerable, to be said by tradition to have been the staff of some famous man, who happened to stick it in the ground, and it took root.

A fellow without money, having 170 miles to travel, fastened a chain and padlock to his legs and lay down to sleep in a field. He was apprehended and carried gratis to a gaol in the town whither he desired to go.

Among other of the woman's jewels was one in
form of a cornucopia, set with 5 rose diamonds
and 12 table diamonds

A ring of a burning heart, set with diamonds.
A jewel in form of a butterfly; two pendants
the Moor's heads ————

A scold and a blockhead — brimstone and
wood — a good match. ————

~~To awaken the sympathies of a person
~~~~ while to enter into this
feeling and sensibility.~~

X To make one's own reflection in a mirror the
subject of a story.

An old volume in a large library — every one
to be afraid to unclasp and open it, because
it was said to be a book of magic

In a dream, to wander to some place where
may be heard the complaints of all the miserable on earth. ————
+————

A field to be manured in an unexpected
spot, and then to raise flowers there, not knowing what made them so rich and beautiful —
the flowers to have some allusion to the event.

A ghost seen by moonlight — when the moon
was out, it would shine and melt through the
airy substance of a ghost, as through a cloud.

Some common quality, or circumstance, that should
bring together people the most unlike in all other respect, and make a brotherhood or sisterhood of them;
they vile and proud finding themselves in the same category with the mean and despised.

A person to consider himself as the prime mover of certain remarkable events but to discover that
his actions have not contributed in the least thereto.
Another person to be the cause, without suspecting
it. + + + + + + +

A person, or family, long desiring some particular
good; — at last it comes in such profusion as to be
even the great plague of their lives.

Among some of Denmark's jewels was one in form of a
cornucopia, set with 6 rose diamonds and 12 table diamonds
    A ring of a burning heart, set with diamonds
    A jewel in form of a butterfly; two pendants like lion's heads

    A scold and a blockhead—brimstone and wood—a good match.

    [*Entry inked out; possible reading as follows:* To [   ] the
[   ] of a [   ]; and [   ] enter into
their feelings and consciousness.]

    To make one's own reflection in a mirror the subject of a story.

    An old volume in a large library—every one to be afraid to
unclasp and open it, because it was said to be a book of magic

    In a dream, to wander to some place where may be heard the
complaints of all the miserable on earth.

    A girl's lover to be buried in an unsuspected spot, and she to
raise flowers there, not knowing what made them so rich and
beautiful—the flowers to have some allusion to the event.

    A ghost seen by moonlight—when the moon was out, it would
shine and melt through the airy substance of a ghost, as through a
cloud.

    Some common quality, or circumstance, that should bring
together people the most unlike in all other respects, and make a
brotherhood or sisterhood of them; the rich and proud finding
themselves in the same category with the mean and despised.

    A person to consider himself as the prime mover of certain
remarkable events, but to discover that his actions have not
contributed in the least thereto. Another person to be the cause,
without suspecting it.

    A person, or family, long desires some particular good;—at last it
comes in such profusion as to become the great plague of their lives.

It was, perhaps, with a presentiment that he should make his fortune by some singular means, and an eager longing so to do. While digging or boring for water, he strikes upon a salt-spring:

———

To have one event operate in several places—as, for example, if a man's head were to be cut off in one town, men's heads to drop off in several other towns.

———

Follow out the fantasy of a person's taking his life by instalments, instead of at one payment—say ten years of life alternately with ten years of suspended animation.

———

Sentiments in a foreign language, which merely convey, to the sentiment, without retaining, to the reader, any graces of style, or harmony of sound, have somewhat of the charm of thoughts in one's own mind, that have not yet been put into words. No possible words, that we might adapt to them, would realise the unshaped beauty that they appear to possess. This is the reason that translations are never satisfactory;—and less so, I should think, to one who cannot, than who can, pronounce the language.

———

A person to be writing a tale, and to find that it shapes itself against his intentions; that the characters act otherwise than he thought; that an unforeseen event occurs; and a catastrophe which he strives in vain to avert. It might shadow forth his own fate—he having made himself one of the personages.

———

De Lamartine says, that many Polish and European Jews dwell near the lake of Galilee; while they have come, in the decline of life, that they may at least die in the country of their ancestors.

Make an article from Thacher's Medical Biography

A man, perhaps with a presentiment that he shall make his fortune by some singular means, and an eager longing so to do. While digging or boring for water, he strikes upon a salt-spring.

To have one event operate in several places—as, for example, if a man's head were to be cut off in the town, men's heads to drop off in several other towns.

Follow out the fantasy of a person's taking his life by instalments, instead of at one payment—say ten years of life alternately with ten years of suspended animation.

Sentiments in a foreign language, which merely conveys the sentiment, without retaining, to the reader, any graces of style, or harmony of sound, have somewhat of the charm of thoughts in one's own mind, that we /ₐhave/ not yet put into words. No possible words, that we might adapt to them, could realize the unshaped beauty that they appear to possess. This is the reason that translations are never satisfactory;—and less so, I should think, to one who cannot, than who can, pronounce the language.

A person to be writing a tale, and to find that it shapes itself against his intentions; that the characters act otherwise than he thought; that unforeseen events occur; and a catastrophe which he strives in vain to avert. It might shadow forth his own fate—he having made himself one of the personages.

De Lamartine says, that many Polish and German Jews dwell near the lake of Galilee, whither they have come, in the decline of life, that they may at least die in the country of their ancestors.

Make an article from Thacher's Medical Biography

An article on Magazines.
— — —

A history of modes of punishment, ancient
and modern.

A turnpike in America is often of the kind. The first MacAdamizer
X Slacking a high road from Philadelphia to Lancaster, an English gentleman, Mr. John Cunyer, constructed it with first a bottom X common on
earth; then a concave layer, about eighteen
inches deep, of stones about the bigness of a
man's fist. American annual Reg. for 1796.
It is stated as having been done about three years
before. It had first been attempted to make the
road, by laying a foundation of the largest
stones that could be found, and then putting
earth upon them, which being washed away
by rain, the horse's legs would sink through the
stones, and be broken. 1500 £ per mile. It was
sure that the road would last for centuries.
Thus it lasted till now.

X John Ziska a leader of the Hussites, ordered his skin to be made (after death) into
a drum-covering — — —

It is a singular thing, that, at the distance away
of five feet, the work of the greatest dunce looks
just as well as that of the greatest genius — that
little space being all the distance between genius and stupidity.

— To contribute in any thing
The King of England is never more than half
an Englishman X (To give a statement of the
foreign intermixtures of the English King, as
far back as the Alfred of the country.) All
the blood in Europe is in his veins — a mongrel of
the great breeds in all the countries. But in this
contrast with the American rule, that the President shall be native — but on in this

though it would not be
amiss, in these days, that
there should

An article on Magazines.

An history of modes of punishment, ancient and modern.

/A in Eng" in A. instead of in Aen" in E. the first McAdamizer/
Making a high road from Philadelphia to Lancaster, an English gentleman, Mr John Curwen, constructed it with first a bottom of common earth; then a concave layer, about eighteen inches deep, of stones about the bigness of a man's fist. *American Annual Reg,* for 1796. It is stated as having been done about three years before. It had first been attempted to make the road, by laying a foundation of the largest stones that could be found, and then heaping earth upon them; which being washed away by rain, the horses' legs would sink through the stones, and be broken. 1500 £ per mile. It was said that the road would last for centuries.— Has it lasted till now.

John Ziska, a leader of the Hussites, ordered his skin to be made (after death) into a drum-covering.

It is a singular thing, that, at the distance say of five feet, the work of the greatest dunce looks just as well as that of the greatest genius—that little space being all the distance between genius and stupidity.

/No Yankee blood in any King—/though it would not be amiss, in these days, that there should
The King of England is never more than half an Englishman. (To give a statement of the foreign intermixture of the English Kings, as far back as the [genesis] of the crowns.) All the blood in Europe in his veins—a mongrel of the worst breeds in all the countries. But in this contrast with the American rule, that the President shall be native;— but so is the King.

Mrs. Sigourney says, after Coleridge, that "poetry has been its own exceeding great reward." For the writing, perhaps — but would it be so for the reading? — . —

Fine precepts; — to break off custom — to shake off spirits ill-disposed — to meditate on youth — to do nothing against a man's genius.

August 31st 1836. A walk yesterday, down to the shore, near the hospital. Standing on the old grassy battery, that forms a semi-circle round the battery, and looking sea-ward. The sun not a great way above the horizon, yet so far as to give a very golden brightness, when it shone out. Clouds in the vicinity of the sun, and nearly all the rest of the sky covered with clouds, in masses; not a gray uniformity of cloud. A fresh breeze blowing from the land to seaward; if it had been blowing from the sea, it would have raised it in heavy billows, and dashed it to dark brightly against the rocks. But now, the surface of the sea were not at all commoved with billows; — there were only waves enough to take off the gleam, and give it the aspect of iron, after cooling. The clouds above added to the bleak appearance. A few sea birds flitting over the sea-foam, only visible at moments, when they turned their white under-parts towards one; as if they were then just created. The sunshine had a singular effect. The clouds would interpose in such a manner, that some objects seem shaded from it, while others were strongly illuminated. Some of the islands lay in the shade, dark and gloomy; while others kept like things, and discovered spots, or the dark sea and beneath the dark sky. The white light-house sometimes very cheerfully marked. There

Mrs. Sigourney says, after Coleridge, that 'poetry has been its own exceeding great reward.' For the writing, perhaps—but would it be so for the reading?

Four precepts;— to break off custom—to shake off spirits ill-disposed—to meditate on youth—to do nothing against a man's genius.

August 31st, 1836.

A walk yesterday, down to the shore, near the hospital. Standing on the old grassy battery, that forms a semi-circle round the battery, and looking sea-ward. The sun not a great way above the horizon, yet so far as to give a very golden brightness, when it shone out. Clouds in the vicinity of the sun, and nearly all the rest of the sky covered with clouds, in masses; not a gray uniformity of cloud. A fresh breeze blowing from the land to seaward; if it had been blowing from the sea, it would have raised it in heavy billows, and caused it to dash high against the rocks. But now, the surface of the sea was not at all commoved with billows; there was only roughness enough to take off the gleam, and give it the aspect /‸of/ iron, after cooling. The clouds above added to the black appearance. A few sea birds flitting over the surface, only visible at moments, when they turned their white under parts towards me; as if they were then just created. The sunshine had a singular effect. The clouds would interpose in such a manner, that some objects were shaded from it, while others were strongly illuminated. Some of the islands lay in the shade, dark and gloomy; while others seemed like sunny and favored spots, on the dark sea and beneath the dark sky. The white light-houses sometimes very cheerfully marked. There was a schooner about a mile from the shore, at anchor, laden with lumber apparently. The sea all about her had the black iron aspect which I have described; but the vessel herself was brightly illuminated. Hull, masts and spars, were all gilded; and the rigging was made of golden threads. A small white streak of foam breaking around her bows, whilst towards the wind. The shadowiness of the clouds over head made the effect of the sunlight strange when it fell.

A small natural reservoir of water, far above low-water mark, in which I have observed tadpoles always swimming about.

The elm trees have golden branches in tennis—filled with their green, already; and hard on the first of the month (Sept.)

To picture the predicament of worldly people, if admitted to Paradise

John Knox's "First Blast of the Trumpet against the monstrous Regiment of Women.

As the architecture of a country always follows the earliest structures, American architecture should be a refinement of the log-house. The Egyptian is that of stone oven and mound; the Chinese of the tent; the Gothic of over-arching trees. Greek a cabin.

Sir William Berkeley, governor of Virginia, had been fellow of Merton College Oxford. He had travelled much, and was greatly valued for the knowledge which he had acquired. He was expelled by the Parliamentarians from his fellowship. First went to Virginia, in 1646, on public affairs.

"Though we speak nonsense, God will pick out the meaning of it." On extempore prayer, by Hooman, a New England divine.

was a schooner about a mile from the shore, at anchor, laden with
lumber apparently. The sea all about her had the black iron aspect
which I have described; but the vessel herself was brightly illuminated.
Hull, masts, and spars, were all gilded; and the rigging was made of
golden threads. A small white streak of foam breaking around her
bows, [which] towards the wind. The shadowiness of the clouds over
head made the effect of the sunlight strange where it fell.

A small natural reservoir of water, far above low-water mark, in
which I have observed tomcods always swimming about.

The elm trees have golden branches intermingled with their
green, already; and had so the first of the month (Sept.)

To picture the predicament of worldly people, if admitted to
Paradise.

John Knox's 'First Blast of the Trumpet against the monstrous
Regiment of Women.

As the architecture of a country always follows the earliest
structures, American architecture should be a refinement of the
log-house. The Egyptian is so of the cavern and mound; the Chinese
of the tent; the Gothic of over-arching trees. Greek a cabin.

Sir William Berkely, governor of Virginia, had been fellow of
Merton College Oxford. He had travelled much, and was greatly
valued for the knowledge which he had acquired. He was expelled by
the Parliamentarians from his fellowship. First sent to Virginia, in
1646, on public affairs.

"Though we speak nonsense, God will pick out the meaning of
it." On extempore prayer, by Horsman, a New-England divine.

In old times, it must have been much less customary than now, to drink pure water. Walker emphatically mentions, among the sufferings of a clergyman's wife and family, in the great rebellion, that they were forced to drink water, with crab-apples steeped in it, to relish it.

Edward Rawson, Parliamentarian incumbent of the living of Horsmanden, Kent. Walker calls him a New-England man. A Secretary of Massachusetts-bay bore this name. He lost his living, at the Restoration.

Prideaux, Bishop of Worcester, during the sway of the Parliament, was forced to support himself and his family by selling his furniture &c. A friend asked him, "how doth your lordship do?" "Never better in my life," said the bishop; only I have too great a stomach; for I have eaten that little Plate which the sequestrators left me; I have eaten a great library of excellent books; I have eaten a great deal of linen, much of my brass, some of my pewter; and now I am come to eat iron; and what will come next, I know not."

Mr. Kirby, author of a work on the History, Habits, and Instincts of Animals, questions whether there may not be an abyss of waters within the globe, communicating with the ocean; and whether the huge animals of the Saurian tribes, great reptiles supposed to be exclusively antediluvian and now extinct, may not be inhabitants of it. He quotes a passage

In old times, it must have been much less customary than now, to drink pure water. Walker emphatically mentions, among the sufferings of a clergyman's wife and family, in the great rebellion, that they were 'forced to drink water with crab-apples stamped in it, to relish it.'

Edward Rawson, Parliamentarian incumbent of the living of Horsmanden, Kent. Walker calls him a New-England man. A secretary of Massachusetts-bay bore this name. He lost his living, at the Restoration

Prideaux, Bishop of Worcester, during the sway of the Parliament, was forced to support himself and his family by selling his furniture &. A friend asked him, 'how doth your lordship do?' 'Never better in my life,' said the bishop, 'only I have too great a stomach; for I have eaten that little Plate which the sequestrators left me; I have eaten a great library of excellent books; I have eaten a great deal of linen, much of my brass, some of my pewter; and now I am come to eat iron; and what will come next, I know not.'

Mr. Kirby, author of a work on the History, Habits, and Instincts of Animals, questions whether there may not be an abyss of waters within the globe, communicating with the ocean; and whether the huge animals of the saurian tribe, great reptiles supposed to be exclusively antedeluvian and now extinct, may not be inhabitants of it. He quotes a passage from Revelations, where the creatures under the earth are spoken of as distinct from those of the sea; and speaks of a saurian fossil that has been found deep in the subterranean regions. He thinks (or suggests) that these may be the dragons of Scripture.

A poodle-dog, trained by Prof. Blumenbach at Gottingen, hatched hen's eggs, and took a motherly care of the chickens, attending on them and providing their food.

The elephant is not particularly sagacious in the wild state; but becomes so when tamed. The fox directly the contrary, and likewise the wolf.

Modern Jewish Adage:—"Let a man clothe himself beneath his ability; his children according to his ability; and his wife above his ability."

It is said of the eagle, that, in however long a flight, he is never seen to clap his wings to his sides. He seems to govern his movements by the inclination of his wings and tail to the wind, as a ship is propelled by the action of the breeze on her sails.

In old country houses in England, in stead of glass for windows, they used wicker or fine strips of oak, disposed chequerwise. Horn was also used. The windows of princes and great noblemen of chrystal; those of Stodley castle, tho burnished says, of beryl. There were seldom chimneys; and they cooked their meats by a fire made against an iron back, in the great hall. Houses, often of gentry, were built of a heavy timber-frame, filled up with lath and plaster.

from Revelations, where the creatures under the earth are spoken of as distinct from those of the sea; and speaks of a saurian fossil that has been found deep in the subterranean regions. He thinks (or suggests) that these may be the dragons of Scripture

A poodle-dog, trained by Prof. Blumenbach at Gottingen, hatched hen's eggs, and took a motherly care of the chickens, attending on them and providing them food.

The elephant is not particularly sagacious in the wild state, but becomes so when tamed; the fox directly the contrary, and likewise the wolf.

Modern Jewish Adage.— "Let a man clothe himself beneath his ability; his children according to his ability; and his wife above his ability"

It is said of the eagle, that, in however long a flight, he is never seen to clap his wings to his sides. He seems to govern his movements by the inclination of his wings and tail to the wind, as a ship is propelled by the action of the breeze on her sails.

In old country houses in England, instead of glass for windows, they used wicker or fine strips of oak, disposed checkerwise. Horn was also used. The windows of princes and great noblemen of chrystal; those of Studley castle, Hollinshed says, of beryl. There were seldom chimneys; and they cooked their meals by a fire made against an iron back, in the great hall. Houses, often of gentry, were built of a heavy timber-frame, filled up with lath and plaster.

People slept on rough mats or straw pallets, with a round log for a pillow:— Seldom better beds,— than a mattress, with a sack of chaff for a pillow.

October 25th 1836. Saw all yesterday through Dark Lane, and home through the village that of Danvers. Landscape now wholly autumnal. Saw an elderly man, laden with two dry, yellow, rustling bundles of Indian-corn stalks — a good personification of Autumn. Another man hoeing up potatoes, while rows of cabbages lay ripening. Field of dry Indian corn. The grass has still considerable of greenness. Wild rose bushes devoid of leaves, with their deep bright red seed-vessels. Meeting-house in Danvers seen at a distance, with the sun shining through the windows of its belfrey. Barberry bushes, the leaves now of a brown red, still juicy and healthy; very few berries remaining; mostly frost-bitten and wilted. All among the red free grass, dry stalks of weeds &c &c the scream of turkies occasionally seen flying through the sunny air.

In this dismal and squalid chamber, fame was won.

The Abyssinians, after dressing their hair, sleep with their heads in a forked stick, in order not to discompose it.

At the battle of Edge hill (Oct 29th 1642) Capt John Smith, a Nedeaf no [?], capt. Lieut, to Lord James Stuarts horse, with only a groom, attacked three Parliament officers, then enemies, and three Cavaliers, and rescued the royal standard; which they had taken and were guarding; Also slew the Parliamentarian Piell. Cont Mag. 1834—2.

Stephen Gosson supposes robbers, that the bodies of Adam & Eve, before the Fall, were clothed in robes of light; which vanished after their sin

People slept on rough mats or straw pallets, with a round log for a pillow:— seldom better beds than a mattress, with a sack of chaff for a pillow.

October 25th. 1836.

A walk yesterday through Dark Lane, and home through the village street of Danvers. Landscape now wholly autumnal. Saw an elderly man, laden with two dry, yellow, rustling bundles of Indian-corn stalks—a good personification of Autumn. Another man hoeing up potatoes, while rows of cabbages lay ripening. Fields of dry Indian corn. The grass has still considerable of greenness. Wild rose bushes devoid of leaves, with their deep bright-red seed-vessels. Meeting-house in Danvers seen at a distance, with the sun shining through the windows of its belfrey. Barberry bushes, the leaves now of a brown red, still juicy and healthy; very few berries remaining, mostly frost-bitten and wilted. All among the yet green grass, dry stalks of weeds &c. The down of thistles, occasionally seen flying through the sunny air.

In this dismal and squalid chamber, <u>fame</u> was won.

The Abyssinians, after dressing their hair, sleep with their heads in a forked stick, in order not to discompose it.

At the battle of Edge hill (Oct. 23^d 1642) Capt John Smith, a soldier of note—, Capt. Lieut, to Lord James Stuart's horse, with only a groom, attacked a Parliament officer, three cuirassiers, and three arquebusiers, and rescued the royal standard, which they had taken and were guarding. Was this the Virginian Smith. Gent Mag. 1834— 2^d.

Stephen [Graves] supposed, that the bodies of Adam & Eve, before the Fall, were clothed in robes of light; which vanished after their sin.

Lord Chancellor Clare, toward the close of his life, went to a village church, where he might not be known, to partake of the Sacrament.

A man, to escape detection for some offence, ingames a woman whom he has loved in some cavern or other secret haunt. He gradually becomes cruel to her, and feels a loathing delight in his cruelty. She comes to hate him, and loses all her intellect and sensibility, except their hatred. They show an example how the damned, who have partaken of guilt, shall mutually wreak vengeance hereafter. In the catastrophe, the hidden person is discovered.

A missionary to the heathen in a great city, to describe his labors, in the manner of a foreign missionary. —

A satirical article might out of the idea of an imaginary museum, containing such articles as Aaron's rod, the petticoat of General Harrison, the pistol with which Benton shot Jackson;—then a Diorama, consisting of political or other scenes; or done in wax-work. The idea to be wrought out and extended. Perhaps it might be the museum of a deceased old man.

A satire might be made respecting various kinds of ruin — ruin in respect to property — ruin of health — ruin of habits, as drunkenness and all kinds of debauchery — ruin of character, while prosperous in other respects — ruin of the soul. Ruin, perhaps, might be personified as a demon, seizing its victims by various holds.

Those who are very difficult in choosing wives, seem as if they would cut more of Nature's ready-made articles, but want a woman manufactured purposely to their order.

An article on fire — on smoke. Diseases of the mind and soul — even more curious than bodily, diseases.

Lord Chancellor Clare, towards the close of his life, went to a village church, where he might not be known, to partake of the Sacrament.

A man, to escape detection for some offence, immures a woman whom he has loved in some cavern or other secret place. He gradually becomes cruel to her; and feels a loathing delight in his cruelty. She comes to hate him; and loses all her intellect and sensibility, except this hatred. They show an example how the damned, who have partaken of guilt, shall mutually wreak vengeance hereafter. In the catastrophe, the hidden person is discovered.

A missionary to the heathen in a great city. To describe his labors, in the manner of a foreign mission.

A satiral article might out of the idea of an imaginary museum, containing such articles as Aaron's rod, the petticoat of General Harrison, the pistol with which Benton shot Jackson;— then a Diorama, consisting of political or other scenes; or done in wax-work. The idea to be wrought out and extended. Perhaps it might the museum of a deceased old man.

An article might be made respecting various kinds of ruin—ruin as respects property—ruin of health—ruin of habits, as drunkenness and all kinds of debauchery—ruin of character, while prosperous in other respects—ruin of the soul. Ruin perhaps might be personified as a demon, seizing its victims by various holds.

Those who are very difficult in choosing wives, seem as they would take none of Nature's ready-made articles, but want a woman manufactured purposely to their order

An article on fire—on smoke.

Diseases of the mind and soul—even more common than bodily, diseases.

A cave: kindled by one's in a chimney,
and dried them like beans. A mighty life
introduced incidentally, in telling the fate
of the personages of a tale —

A council of the inhabitants of a street,
called by somebody to decide about some
point important to him.

A person, a great mover — some way or other,
to be the means of introducing some terrible pestilence into the world — as the small-pox.

All sorts of persons, and every individual has a
place to fill in the world, and is important in
some respects, whether he chooses to be so or not.
Fortune in the gold mine, and bachelor — the aged
person — the infant, — the idiot — even the drunkard — et cetera.

A young couple take up their residence in a
retired street of a large town, there decay, then
successive several of the neighbors, and
thence turn the dead body of her husband.

A Thanksgiving Dinner — all the miserable on earth are to be invited: — as, the drunkard, the prostitute, the bereaved parent, the
ruined merchant, the broken-hearted lover, the
poor widow, the old woman or man, who
have outlived their generation, the disappointed author, the wounded, sick, and broken
soldier, the diseased person, the infidel,
the man with an evil conscience, little & then
children, or with neglectful parents, shall be admitted to the table; and many others. The giver
of the feast goes out to deliver his invitations;
some of the guests he meets in the street, some
he knocks at the doors of their houses, &c.
The description must be rather. But who
must be the giver of the feast, and what
his claims to preside? A man who has never
found out what he is fit for, who has no
settled aim or object in life, and whom
mind preys him, making him the sufferer of
every kinds of misery, he should seek some
poor old sorrowful person, with worn out
and calamities than any other, and entitle her &
with a reflection that perchance would make
all that miserable company truly thankful.
&c.

A man smothered by smoke in a chimney, and dried there like bacon. It might be introduced incidentally, in telling the fates of the personages of a tale

A Council of the inhabitants of a street, called by somebody to decide upon some point important to him.

A person, a great sinner in some way or other, to be the means of introducing some terrible pestilence into the world—as the small-pox.

All sorts of persons, and every individual has a place to fill in the world, and is important in some respects, whether he chooses to be so or not. Instance in the old maid and bachelor—the aged person—the infant,—the idiot—even the drunkard—et cetera.

A young couple take up their residence in a retired street of a large town. One day, she summons several of the neighbors in, and shows them the dead body of her husband

A Thanksgiving Dinner—all the miserable on earth are to be invited:—as, the drunkard, the prostitute, the bereaved parent, the ruined merchant, the broken-hearted lover, the poor widow, the old woman or man, who have outlived their generation, the disappointed author, the wounded, sick, and broken soldier, the diseased person, the infidel, the man with an evil conscience, little orphan children, or with neglectful parents, shall be admitted to the table; and many others. The giver of the feast goes out to deliver his invitations; some of the guests he meets in the streets; some he knocks at the doors of their houses for. The description must be rapid. But who must be the giver of the feast, and what his claims to preside? A man who has never found out what he is fit for, who has no settled aim or object in life, and whose mind gnaws him, making him the sufferer of many kinds of misery. He should meet some pious old sorrowful person, with more outward calamities than any other, and invite him, with a reflection that piety would make all that miserable company truly thankful.

Merry — in Merry England — does not mean mirthful; but is corrupted from an old Teutonic word, signifying famous, or renowned.

In an old London advertisement 1678, there is an advertisement, among other goods at auction, of a Black Girl about 15 years old to be sold.

Tarleton, of the Revolution, is said to have been one of the two handsomest men in Europe — the prince of Wales (afterwards George IV) being the other. Some authorities, however, have represented him as ungainly in person, and coarse in manners. Tarleton was originally bred to the law, and was to be a Merchant of Liverpool, but quitted for the army early in life, born in 1754. Wrote his own memoirs after returning from America. Afterwards in Parliament. Never afterwards distinguished in arms. Created baronet in 1818; and died childless in 1833. Thought he was not sufficiently honored among more modern heroes. Lost hand of his right hand. His battles & ——— are in ———

It would be a good idea for a painter to paint a picture of a great actor, representing him in several different characters of one scene — as Iago and Othello, for instance.

In the tenth century, mechanism of organs or clerk of that one in Westminster Abbey, with 400 pipes, required 26 bellows and 70 stout men. First organ known in Europe, made by King Pepin from Emperor Constantine Copronymus, in 757. Water body was kept in reservoir under the pipes; and the keys being struck, valves of pipes opened, and steam rushed through with noise. The trouble of working them thus, was lost. Then came bellows. Organs first built in Germany.

After the siege of Sebastopol, the children played wherever in the street, with grape and cannon to shoot

A shell, in falling, buries itself in the earth; and when it explodes, a large pit is made by the earth being blown about in all directions; — sometimes large enough to hold 3 or more cart-loads of earth. The holes are somewhat

Merry—in Merry England—does not mean mirthful; but is corrupted from an old Teutonic word, signifying famous, or renowned

In an old London newspaper 1678, there is an an advertisement, among other goods at auction, of a Black Girl about 15 years old to be sold.

Tarleton, of the Revolution, is said to have been one of the two handsomest men in Europe—the prince of Wales (afterwards George IV) being the other. Some authorities, however, have represented him as ungainly in person, and rough in manners. Tarleton was originally bred to the law, and was son to the Mayor of Liverpool, but quitted for the army early in life; born in 1754 /of ancient family/. Wrote his own memoirs after returning from America. Afterwards in Parliament. Never afterwards distinguished in arms. Created Baronet—1818, and died childless in 1833. Thought he was not sufficiently honored among more modern heroes. /Lost part of his right hand at battle of Guildford Court-House. A man of pleasure in England/

It would be a good idea for a painter to paint a picture of a great actor, representing him in several different characters of one scene—as Iago and Othello, for instance.

In the tenth century, mechanism of organs so clumsy, that one in Westminster abbey, with 400 pipes, required 26 bellows and 70 stout men. First organ ever known in Europe, rec'd by King Pepin from Emperor Constantine Copronymus, in 757. Water boiling was kept in reservoir under the pipes; and the keys being struck, valves of pipes opened, and steam rushed through with noise. The secret of working them thus, was lost. Then came bellows-organs; first Louis le Debonnaire.

After the siege of Antwerp, the children played marbles in the streets, with grape and cannister shot.

A shell, in falling, buries itself in the earth; and when it explodes, a large pit is made by the earth being blown about in all directions;— sometimes large enough to hold 3 or 4 cart-loads of earth. The holes are circular

A French artilleryman being buried in his military cloak in the ramparts, — a shell exploded and unburied him. —

In the Netherlands, to form hedges, young trees are interwoven into a sort of lattice-work; and in time they grow together at the points of junction, so that the fence is all of one piece. —

To show the effect of gratified revenge — as an instance, merely, suppose a woman sues her owner for breach of promise, and gets the money by installments, thro' a long series of years. At last, when the miserable victim was utterly trodden down, this treasure would have become a very devil of evil passions, — they having overgrown his whole nature, — so that a far greater evil would have come upon himself than on his victim. —

Adventures of a bell — in a Roman Catholic chapel (Father Ralli's) &c. The tale would admit of a good deal of historic picturesqueness.

We sometimes congratulate ourselves, at the moment of waking from a troubled dream; it may be so, the moment after death.

Anciently, when long-buried bodies were found undecayed in the grave, a species of sanctity was attributed to them.

The father of Earl Grey was General Grey, known in our Revolution.

Some chimneys of ancient halls used to be swept by firing a culverin up them.

At Leith, in 1711, a glass bottle was blown, of the capacity of two English bushels.

The buff and blue of the Union were adopted by Fox and the whigs — pretty in England. The Prince of Wales wore them.

A French artilleryman being buried in his military cloak on the ramparts, a shell exploded and unburied him—

In the Netherlands, to form hedges, young trees are interwoven into a sort of lattice-work; and in time, they grow together at the points of junction, so that the fence is all of one piece

To show the effect of gratified revenge—as an instance, merely, suppose a woman sues her lover for breach of promise, and gets the money by instalments, thro' a long series of years. At last, when the miserable victim was utterly trodden down, the triumpher would have become a very devil of evil passions,—they having overgrown his whole nature; so that a far greater evil would have come upon himself, than on his victim.

Adventures of a bell as in a Roman Catholic chapel (Father Ralle's) &c. The tale would admit of a good deal of historic picturesqueness.

We sometimes congratulate ourselves, at the moment of waking from a troubled dream; it may be so, the moment after death.

Anciently, when long-buried bodies were found undecayed in the grave, a species of sanctity was attributed to them.

The father of Earl Grey was General Grey, known in our Revolution.

Some chimneys of ancient halls used to be swept by firing a culverin up them

At Leith, in 1711, a glass bottle was blown, of the capacity of two English bushels.

The buff and blue of the Union were adopted by Fox and the whig-party in England. The Prince of Wales wore them.

In 1621, a Mr. Copinger left a certain charity (an alms-house) of which four poor persons were to partake, after the death of his eldest son and his wife. It was a tenement and yard. The person, headborough, and his five other sons were to appoint the persons. At the time specified, however, all but one of his sons were dead; and he was in such poor circumstances, that he obtained the benefit of the charity for himself, as one of the four.

A Town-Clerk arranges the punishments that are given in, according to his own judgment.

To make a story from Robert Raikes seeing dirty children at play in streets of London, and enquiring of a woman about them. She tells him that on Sundays, when they were not employed, they were a great deal worse — making the street like hell, screeching at church &c. There he was ordered to employ women at a shilling to teach them on Sundays; and thus Sunday schools were established.

To rehearse the different departments of United States government by village functionaries. The war-department, watchman — the law, constable & the merchants, a variety store &c.

The race of mankind to be swept away, leaving all their cities &c and works. Then another human pair to be placed in the world, with certain intelligence, like Adam and Eve, but knowing nothing of their predecessors, or of their own history and destiny. They perhaps to be des-

In 1621, a Mr. Copinger left a certain charity (an alms-house) of which four poor persons were to partake, after the death of his eldest son and his wife. It was a tenement and yard. The parson, headboroughs, and his five other sons were to appoint the persons. At the time specified, however, all but one of his sons were dead; and he was in such poor circumstances, that he obtained the benefit of the charity for himself, as one of the four.

A Town-Clerk arranges the publishments that are given in, according to his own judgment.

To make a story from Robert Raikes seeing dirty children at play in streets of London, and enquiring of a woman about them. She tells him that on Sundays, when they were not employed, they were a great deal worse—making the street like hell, playing at chuck &c. There he was induced to employ women at a shilling to teach them on Sundays; and thus Sunday schools were established.

To represent the different departments of United States government by village functionaries. The war-department, watchman—the law, constable—the merchants, a variety-store &c.

The race of mankind to be swept away, leaving all their cities &c. and works. Then another human pair to be placed in the world, with mature intelligence, like Adam and Eve, but knowing nothing of their predecessors, or of their own nature and destiny. They perhaps to be des-

seided as working out this knowledge, by their
sympathy with what they knew, and by their
own feelings. —

Memorials of the family of Haythorne
in the church of the village of Dundry,
Somersetshire (Eng.); — the church is ancient
and small, but has a prodigiously high
tower, of more modern date, being erected
in the time of Edw. IV. It serves as a
landmark for an amazing extent.

At the expiration of the Bloody Mass, a man,
coming into a house, sounded three times
with his mouth, like a trumpet, and then
made proclamation to the family. A bonfire was built, and little children were
made to carry wood to it, that they might
remember the circumstances in old age. Meat
and drink provided at the bonfire.

To describe a boyish combat with
snow-balls; and the victorious leader to
have a statue of snow erected to him.
A statue on ambition and fame to be
made out of this idea. It might be a
child's story.

One ought to be possessed by two different
spirits; so that half of the essay shall
express one mood, and the other half another.

An old English gentleman desirous to
have a feast-daily shirt. to keep a good table, and to said between the tables without ever working and

cribed as working out this knowledge, by their sympathy with what they saw, and by their own feelings.

Memorials of the family of Haythorne in the church of the village of Dundry, Somersetshire, (Eng.);—the church is ancient and small, but has a prodigiously high tower, of more modern date, being erected in the time of Edw. IV. It serves as a landmark for an amazing extent.

At the accession of the Bloody Mary, a man, coming into a house, sounded three times with his mouth, like a trumpet, and then made proclamation to the family. A bonfire was built, and little children were made to carry wood to it, that they might remember the circumstance in old age. Meat and drink provided at the bonfire.

To describe a boyish combat with snow-balls, and the victorious leader to have a statue in snow erected to him. A satire on ambition and fame to be made out of this idea. It might be a child's story.

One body to be possessed by two different spirits; so that half of the visage shall express one mood, and the other half another

An old English sea-captain desires to have a fast-sailing ship, to keep a good table, and to sail between the tropics without ever making land

A singular fact, that when man is a brute, he is the most sensual and loathsome of all brutes.

A snake taken into a man's stomach, and nourished there from fifteen years to thirty five — tormenting him most horribly. A type of envy or some other evil passion.

A sketch, illustrating the imperfect compensations which time makes for its devastations on our persons — giving a wreath of laurels while it makes us bald — honors for infirmities — wealth for a broken constitution — and at last, when we have every thing that seems desirable, death strikes us. To contrast the men who have thus reached the summit of ambition, with the ambitious youth.

Walking along the track of the Rail-road, I observed a place where the workmen had bored a hole through the solid rock, in order to blast it; but striking on a spring of water, beneath the rock, it gushed up through the hole. It looked as if the water were contained within the rock.

A Fancy Ball, at which the prominent American writers should appear dressed in character.

A singular fact, that when man is a brute, he is the most sensual and loathsome of all brutes.

A snake taken into a man's stomach; and nourished there from fifteen years to thirty five—tormenting him most horribly. A type of envy or some other evil passion.

A sketch, illustrating the imperfect compensations which time makes for its devastations on our persons—giving a wreath of laurels while it makes us bald—honors for infirmities—wealth for a broken constitution—and at last, when we have every thing that seems desirable, death seizes us. To contrast the man who has thus reached the summit of ambition, with the ambitious youth.

Walking along the track of the rail road, I observed a place where the workmen had bored a hole through the solid rock, in order to blast it; but striking on a spring of water, beneath the rock, it gushed up through the hole. It looked as if the water were contained within the rock.

A Fancy Ball, at which the prominent American writers should appear dressed in character.

A Lament for _Life's_ wasted Sunshine
___

A sick man left, by will, his mansion and
estate to a poor couple. They remove into
it; and find there a darksome tenant,
whom they are forbidden by the will to
turn away. They become wrath; he becomes a torment to them; and in the finale
he turns out to be the former master of the
estate.
~~~

A new classification of Society to be instituted — instead of rich and poor, high and
low, they are to be classed first by their
sorrows: — for instance, whoever there are, whether
in mansion or hovel, who are mourning the
loss of relations and friends, and who wear black,
whether the cloth be coarse or superfine, they
are to make one class; — Secondly, all who
have the same diseases, whether they lie
under damask canopies, or on straw pallets,
or in the wards of hospitals, they are to form
one class; — thirdly, all who are guilty of the
same sins, whether the world knows them or
not, whether they languish in prison, looking
forward to the gallows, or walk honored
among men, they also form one class. Then
proceed to generalize, and classify the whole
world together, as none can claim utter exemption from either sin, sorrow, or disease;
and if they could, yet Death, like a pearl-
Parent, comes and sweeps them all through
one darksome portal — all his children.

Fortune to come like a pedler with her goods: —
a wreath of laurel, diamonds, crowns, selling
them, but asking for them ___ sacrifice of health,
of integrity, perhaps of life in the battle-field,
of the real pleasures of life &c. Who would buy,
if the price were to be paid down.

A lament for Life's wasted Sunshine

A rich man left by will his mansion and estate to a poor couple. They remove into it; and find there a darksome servant, whom they are forbidden by the will to turn away. They become corrupt; he becomes a torment to them; and in the finale, he turns out to be the former master of the estate.

A new classification of society to be instituted—instead of rich and poor, high and low, they are to be classed first by their sorrows:— for instance, wherever there /ₐare/ any, whether in mansion or hovel, who are mourning the loss of relatives and friends, and who wear black, whether the cloth be coarse or superfine, they are to make one class;— secondly, all who have the same diseases, whether they lie under damask canopies, or on straw pallets, or in the wards of hospitals, they are to form one class;— thirdly, all who are guilty of the same sins, whether the world knows them or not, whether they languish in prison, looking forward to the gallows, or walk honored among men, they also form one class. Then proceed to generalize, and classify the whole world together, as none can claim utter exemption from either sin, sorrow, or disease; and if they could, yet Death like a great parent, comes and sweeps them all through one darksome portal—all his children.

Fortune to come like a pedler with his goods;— as wreaths of laurel, diamonds, crowns, selling them, but asking for them the sacrifice of health, of integrity; perhaps of life in the battle-field, of the real pleasures of life &c. Who would buy, if the price were to be paid down.

The dying exclamation of the Emperor Augustus — Has it not been well acted? — An essay on the miseries of being always under a masque — a veil may sometimes be needful, but never a masque. . . . . who wear masques, in all classes of Society, and never take it off, even in the most familiar moments — though sometimes it may chance to slide aside.

"The Frenzied Father." "The Maniac Mother." "The Crazy Child."

The various disguises under which Ruin makes his approaches to his victims — to the merchant, in the guise of a merchant, offering Speculations — to the young heir, a jolly companion — & the maiden, a sighing sentimental lover — to the &c

Alderman, the Indian who shot King Philip, was rewarded with Philip's head; which for a considerable time he carried about, as a show, and made much money thereby.

Persons to be expecting some occurrence, and watching for the two principal Actors in it; and to find that the occurrence was even then happening, and that they themselves are the two actors.

Philip's head was afterwards exposed two & up years on a gibbet at Plymouth: his hands exposed in Boston; his body left unburied.

What were the contents of the Burden of Christian, in the Pilgrim's Progress? He must have been taken for a pedlar, travelling with his pack.

To state, as the sun goes down, what events have happened in the course of the day — events of ordinary occurrence, as the clocks have struck, the dews have been dewed &c.

The dying exclamation of the Emperor Augustus— Has it not been well acted?'— An essay on the misery of being always under a masque—A veil may sometimes be needful, but never a masque. Instances of people who wear masques, in all classes of society, and never take it off even in the most familiar moments—though sometimes it may chance to slip aside.

"The Frenzied Father." "The Maniac Mother," "The Crazy Child."

The various guises under which Ruin makes his approaches to his victims—to the merchant, in the guise of a merchant, offering speculations—to the young heir, a jolly companion—to the maiden a sighing sentimental lover—to the &c.

Alderman, the Indian who shot King Philip, was rewarded with Philip's head; which for a considerable time he carried about as a shew, and made much money thereby.

Two persons to be expecting some occurrence, and watching for the two principal actors in it; and to find that the occurrence is even then passing, and that they themselves are the two actors.

Philip's head was afterwards exposed twenty years on a gibbet at Plymouth; his hands exposed in Boston; his body left unburied

What were the contents of the burden of Christian, in the Pilgrim's Progress? He must have been taken for a pedler, travelling with his pack

To think, as the sun goes down, what events have happened in the course of the day—events of ordinary occurrence. As the clocks have struck, the dead have been buried &c.

curious to imagine what murmurings and discontent would be excited, if any of the great orders of human nature were to be abolished,—as, for instance, Death.—

There is a fund of evil in every human heart, which may remain latent, perhaps through the whole of life; but circumstances may arouse it to activity. To imagine such circumstances. A woman tempted to be false to her husband, apparently through mere whim—a young man to feel an instinctive thirst for blood, and to commit murder; this appetite may be traced in the popularity of criminal trials.— The appetite might be observed first in a child, and then traced afterwards, manifesting itself in various modes to every stage of life.

The good deeds in an evil life—the generous, noble, and excellent actions done by people habitually wicked—what is to become of them.

Trifles to one, are matters of life and death to another. As for instance, a farmer desires a brisk breeze to winnow his grain; and mariners to blow them out of the reach of pirates.

A recluse, like myself, or a prisoner, to measure time by the progress of sunshine through his chamber.—

Would it not be wiser for people to rejoice at all they now sorrow for—and vice versa. To put on bridal garment at funerals, and mourning at weddings. For their friends to condole with them when they attained riches or power, as sully or much care added to.

"Men of cold passions have quick eyes." Bishop Hurd

In a village, it was custom to hang a funeral garland, or other token of death, in a house where some one had died; and then to let it hang till a death occurred elsewhere, and then to hang that same garland over the other house;—it would have, methinks, a strong effect.

Curious to imagine what murmurings and discontent would be excited, if any of the great miseries of human nature were to be abolished,—as, for instance, Death.

There is a fund of evil in every human heart, which may remain latent, perhaps through the whole of life; but circumstances may arouse it to activity. To imagine such circumstances. A woman tempted to be false to her husband, apparently through mere whim—a young man to feel an instinctive thirst for blood, and to commit murder; this appetite may be traced in the popularity of criminal trials— The appetite might be observed first in a child, and then traced upwards, manifesting itself in crimes suited to every stage of life.

The good deeds in an evil life—the generous, noble and excellent actions done by people habitually wicked—what is to become of them.

Trifles to one, are matters of life and death to another. As for instance, a farmer desires a brisk breeze to winnow his grain; and mariners to blow them out of the reach of pirates.

A recluse, like myself, or a prisoner, to measure time by the progress of sunshine through his chamber.

Would it not be wiser for people to rejoice at all they now sorrow for—and vice versa, to put on bridal garments at funerals, and mourning at weddings. For their friends to condole with them, when they attained riches or power, as only so much care added &c.

"Men of cold passions have quick eyes." Bishop Hurd.

If in a village, it were custom to hang a funeral garland, or other token of death, on a house where someone had died; and then to let it hang till a death occurred elsewhere and then to hang that same garland over the other house;—it would have, methinks, a strong effect.

No fountain so small, but that heaven may be imaged in its bosom.

Fame — Some very humble persons in a town may be said to possess it — as the lamp-post, the town crier, the constable &c; and they are known to every body; while many richer, more intellectual, worthier persons are unknown by the majority of their fellow citizens. Something analogous in the world at large.

—　—　—

The ideas of people in general are not raised higher than the roofs of their houses. All their interests extend over the earth's surface, in a layer of that thickness. The meeting-house steeple reaches out of their sphere.

—　—　—

Nobody will use other people's experience, nor has any of his own till it is too late to use it.

—　—　—

A virtuous but giddy girl to attempt to play a trick on a man. He sees what she is about, and contrives matters so, that she throws herself completely into his power, and is ruined — all in jest.

—　—　—

Two lovers to plan the building of a pleasure house on a certain spot of ground; but various meanings occur to prevent it. Once they a group of miserable children there; once it the scene with crime is plotted; at last the dead body of one of the lovers, or of a dear friend, is found there; and instead of the pleasure house, they build him a humble tomb. The moral, that there is no place on earth fit for the site of a pleasure house; because there is no spot that has not been saddened by human grief, stained by crime, or hallowed by death. It might be three friends who plan it, instead of two lovers; and the dearest dies.

No fountain so small, but that Heaven may be imaged in its bosom.

Fame—some very humble persons in a town may be said to possess it:— as the penny-post, the town-crier, the constable &c; and they are known to every body; while many richer, more intellectual, worthier persons are unknown by the majority of their fellow citizens. Something analogous in the world at large.

The ideas of people in general are not raised higher than the roofs of the houses. All their interests extend over the earth's surface, in a layer of that thickness. The meeting-house steeple reaches out of their sphere.

Nobody will use other people's experience, nor has any of his own till it is too late to use it.

A virtuous but giddy girl to attempt to play a trick on a man. He sees what she is about, and contrives matters so, that she throws herself completely into his power, and is ruined—all in jest.

Two lovers to plan the building of a pleasure house on a certain spot of ground; but various seeming accidents prevent it. Once they a group of miserable children there; once it is the scene w/ₐh/ere crime is plotted; at last the dead body of one of the lovers, or of a dear friend, is found there; and instead of the pleasure house, they build him a marble tomb. The moral, that there is no place on earth fit for the site of a pleasure house; because there is no spot that has not been saddened by human grief, stained by crime, or hallowed by death. It might be three friends who plan it, instead of two lovers; and the dearest dies.

A partially insane man to believe himself the provincial governor, or other great official, of ——— Massachusetts. His scene might be the Province House.

Comfort for childless people:— A married couple with ten children have been the means of bringing about ten funerals.

A blind man, one dark night, carried a torch, in order that people might see him, and not run against him, and direct him how to avoid danger.

Dr. Franklin's family were blacksmiths at Ecton, Northamptonshire. (Eng.)

To picture a child's (of four or five years old) reminiscence, at sunset, of a long summer's day — his first awaking, his studies, his sports, his little fits of joy & grief — perhaps a whipping &c. &c.

The Blind Man's Walk.—

(A letter, written a century or more ago, but which has never yet been unsealed

To picture a virtuous family, the different members examples of virtuous disposition in their ways;— then introduce a vicious person, and trace out the relations that arise between him and them, and the manner in which all are effected.

A man to flatter himself with the idea that he would not be guilty of some certain wickedness — as for instance to yield to the personal temptations of the devil — yet to find, ultimately, that he was, at that very time, committing that same wickedness.

A partially insane man to believe himself the provincial governor, or other great official, of Massachusetts. The scene might be the Province-House.

Comfort for childless people;— A married couple with ten children have been the means of bringing about ten funerals.

A blind man, on a dark night, carried a torch, in order that people might see him, and not run against him, and direct him how to avoid dangers.

Dr. Franklin's family were blacksmiths, at Ecton, Northamptonshire. (Eng.)

To picture a child's (of four or five years old) reminiscence, at sunset, of a long sunny summer's day—his first awakening, his studies, his sports, his little fits of passion and grief—perhaps a whipping &c. &c.

The Blind Man's Walk.

A letter, written a century or more ago, but which has never yet been unsealed

To picture a virtuous family, the different members examples of virtuous dispositions in their way;— then introduce a vicious person, and trace out the relations that arise between him and them, and the manner in which all are effected.

A man to flatter himself with the idea that he would not be guilty of some certain wickedness—as for instance to yield to the personal temptations of the devil—yet to find, ultimately, that he was, at that very time, committing that same wickedness.

What would a man do, if he were compelled to live always in the sultry heart of society, and could never bathe himself in cool solitude.

A girl's love to be plain and carnal in her flower garden; and the earth love that over him. That particular spot (which she happens to plant with some peculiar variety of flowers) produces them of admirable splendor, beauty, and perfume; and the delight, with an indescribable impulse, to wear them in her bosom, and have them to be down her chamber. Thus the classic fantasies would be realized, of dead people transformed to flowers.

"Though I sick and crazy be,
Jesus, Jesus died for me!"
                    Elizabeth Heath.

Object seen by a magic lantern, reversed. A street, or other location, might be presented, where there would be opportunity to bring forward all objects of worldly interest; and thus much pleasant satire might be the result.

Insincerity in a man's own heart makes all his enjoyments, all that concerns him unreal; so that his whole life must seem like merely a dramatic representation. And this would be the case, even though he were surrounded by tender-hearted relatives and friends.

What would a man do, if he were compelled to live always in the sultry heat of society, and could never bathe himself in cool solitude.

A girl's lover to be slain and buried in her flower garden; and the earth leveled over him. That particular spot (which she happens to plant with some peculiar variety of flowers) produces them of admirable splendor, beauty, and perfume; and she delights, with an indescribable impulse, to wear them in her bosom, and have them to perfume her chamber. Thus the classic fantasies would be realized, of dead people transformed to flowers.

"Though I sick and crazy lie,
  Jesus, Jesus died for me!"
        Elizabeth Heath.

Objects seen by a magic lantern, reversed. A street, or other location, might be presented, where there would be opportunity to bring forward all objects of worldly interest; and thus much pleasant satire might be the result.

Insincerity in a man's own heart makes all his enjoyments, all that concerns him, unreal; so that his whole life must seem like merely a dramatic representation. And this would be the case, even though he were surrounded by true-hearted relatives and friends.

& Alexander Carter['s?] Anecdote of Lord Treasurer
Weston, in Clarendon's history.

August 22d 1837. A walk yesterday
afternoon down to the Juniper and Three tree
Islands. Singular effect of partial sunshine,
the sky being broadly and heavily clouded, and land and sea, in consequence,
being generally overspread with a sombre gloom. But the sunshine, somehow
or other, found its way between the interstices of the clouds, and illuminated
some of the distant objects very vividly.
The white sails of a ship caught, and
gleamed brilliant as driven snow, her
hull being scarcely visible, and the sea
around dark; other smaller vessels too,
so that they looked like heavenly winged
things, just alighting on a gloomy world.
Shifting their sail, perhaps, or going on another
tack, they almost disappear at once in the
sombre distance. Islands are seen in heavenly
sunshine and green glory, their rocks also sunny, and their white beaches; while other islands,
for no apparent reason, are in deep shade,
and there the gloom of the rest of the world.
Sometimes part of an island is illuminated, and part dark. When the sunshine falls
on a very distant island, nearer ones being in shade, it seems greatly to extend the
bounds of visible space, and put the horizon to a further distance. The sea roughly
rushing against the shore, and plashing s-
against the rocks, and grating back over
the sands. A vessel a little way from the
shore, tossing and pausing at anchor; then
men fishing. Black birds flitting from place to place.
"If I know what good manners is, then I say
them, though I seldom eat any myself."
                        Inland Downeast Yankee

"Remember Caesar"— Anecdote of Lord treasurer Weston, in Clarendon's History.

August 22^d 1837.

A walk yesterday afternoon down to the Junater and Winter Island. Singular effect of partial sunshine, the sky being broadly and heavily clouded, and land and sea, in consequence, being generally over spread with a sombre gloom. But the sunshine, somehow or other, found its way between the interstices of the clouds, and illuminated some of the distant objects very vividly. The white sails of a ship caught, and gleamed brilliant as sunny snow, her hull being scarcely visible, and the sea around dark; other smaller vessels too, so that they looked like heavenly winged things, just alighting on a gloomy world. Shifting their sails, perhaps, or going on another tack, they almost disappear at once in the sombre distance. Islands are seen in summer sunshine and green glory, their rocks also sunny, and their white beaches, while other islands, for no apparent reason, are in deep shade, and share the gloom of the rest of the world. Sometimes part of an island is illuminated, and part dark. When the sunshine falls on a very distant island, nearer ones being /in/ shade, it seems greatly to extend the bounds of visible space, and put the horizon to a farther distance. The sea roughly rushing against the shore, and dashing against the rocks, and grating back over the sands. A boat, a little way from the shore, tossing and swinging at anchor; the men fishing. Beach birds flitting from place to place.

"I know what good manners are when I see them, though I seldom use any myself."

Inland Downeast Yankee

#The family seat of the Hathornes is Wig-
castle, Wigton, Wiltshire. The present head
of the family, now residing there, is Hugh
Hathorne — according to them. William
Hathorne, who came over in 1635-6, was a
younger brother of the family. # or Castlewig? 9

A young man and girl meet together, each
in search of a person to be known by some
particular sign. They watch and wait a great
while for that person to pass; at last some
casual circumstance discloses that each is
the one whom the other is waiting for. Moral,
that what we need for our happiness is often
close at hand, if we knew but how to seek
for it.

The journal of a human heart, in ordinary
circumstances, for a single day. The lights and
shadows that flit across it; its internal vicissitudes. &c

Instinct to be thus exemplified — various
good and desirable things to be presented to
a young man, and offered to his acceptance, —
as a friend, a wife, a fortune — but he to refuse them all, suspecting that it was merely
a delusion. Yet all to be real, and he to
be told so, when too late.

A man tries to be happy in love; he cannot
sincerely give his heart, and the affair seems
like a dream; — in domestic life, the same; —
in politics, a seeming patriot; but still he
is sincere, and all seems like a theatre.

An old man, on a summer day, sits on
a hill-top, or on the observatory of his house,

The family seat of the Hathornes is / # / Wigcastle, Wigton, Wiltshire. The present head of the family, now residing there, is Hugh Hathorne—according to Eben. William Hathorne, who came over in 1635–6, was a younger brother of the family. # or Castlewig?

A young man and girl meet together, each in search of a person to be known by some particular sign. They watch and wait a great while for that person to pass; at last some casual circumstance discloses that each is the one whom the other is waiting for. Moral, that what we need for our happiness is often close at hand, if we knew but how to seek for it.

The journal of a human heart, in ordinary circumstances, for a single day. The lights and shadows that flit across it; its internal vicissitudes &c

Distrust to be thus exemplified—various good and desirable things to be presented to a young man, and offered to his acceptance,— as a friend, a wife, a fortune—but he to refuse them all, suspecting that it was merely a delusion. Yet it all to be real, and he to be told so, when too late.

A man tries to be happy in love; he cannot sincerely give his heart, and the affair seems like a dream;— in domestic life, the same;— in politics, a seeming patriot; but still he is sincere, and all seems like a theatre.

An old man, one summer day, sits on a hill-top, or on the observatory of his house,

and use the sunshine trips from one object to a-
nother, connected with the events of his past
life;— as the school-house—the place where his
wife lived in her maidenhood — its setting
beams falling on the church-yard.

    An idle man's pleasures, and occupa-
tions and thoughts, during a day spent by
the sea-shore:— among them, that of sitting
on the top of a cliff, and throwing stones at
his own shadow, far below.

    A Blind man to set forth on a walk
through ways unknown to him, and to
trust to the guidance of anybody who
would take the trouble;— the different
characters who would undertake it, some
mischievous, some well-meaning but incapable;— perhaps one blind man undertakes
to lead another. At last, possibly, he rejects
all guidance, and blunders on by himself.
Perhaps it might be a blindfolded man,
for a wager.

    In the cabinet of the Essex Historical Soci-
ety, old portraits — Governor Leverett, a dark
countenanced face, the figure two-thirds length,
clothed in a sort of frock-coat, buttoned, and a
broad sword-belt girded round the waist,
and fastened with a large steel buckle;—
the hilt of the sword steel; altogether very
striking. Sir William Pepperell in English
regimentals, coat, waistcoat, and breeches,
all of red broadcloth, richly gold-embroidered; he holds a general's truncheon in
his right hand, and extends his left towards
the batteries erected against Louisburg, —
in the country near which he is standing. Endicott, Pynchon, and others, in skull-caps, & bands &

and sees the sunshine pass from one object to another; connected with the events of his past life—as the school-house—the place where his wife lived in her maidenhood—its setting beams falling on the church-yard.

An idle man's pleasures, and occupations, and thoughts, during a day spent by the sea-shore:— among them, that of sitting on the top of a cliff, and throwing stones at his own shadow, far below.

A Blind man to set forth on a walk through ways unknown to him, and to trust to the guidance of anybody who would take the trouble; the different characters who would undertake it, some mischievous, some well meaning but incapable;— perhaps one blind man undertakes to lead another. At last, possibly, he rejects all guidance, and blunders on by himself. Perhaps it might be a blindfolded man, for a wager.

In the cabinet of the Essex Historical Society, old portraits— governor Leverett, a dark moustachioed face, the figure two-thirds length, clothed in a sort of frock-coat, buttoned, and a broad sword-belt girded round the waist, and fastened with a large steel-buckle:— the hilt of the sword steel; altogether very striking. Sir William Peperell in English regimentals, coat, waistcoat, and breeches all of red broadcloth, richly gold-embroidered; he holds a general's truncheon in his right hand, and extends his left towards the batteries erected against Louisbourg, in the country near which he is standing. Endicott, Pyncheon, and others in scull-caps, braids &c.

Half a dozen, or more, family portraits of
the Olivers, some in plain dresses, brown, crimson, or claret. Others with gorgeous gold
embroidered waistcoats, descending almost
to the knees, so as to form the most conspicuous article of dress. Ladies, with lace
ruffles, the painting of which, in one of the
pictures, cost five guineas. Peter Oliver,
who grew crazy, used to fight with these
family pictures, in the old mansion-house,
and the face and breast of one lady
were cut and stabs inflicted by him.
Miniatures in oil, with the paint peeling off.
of them, old yellow faces. Olivers' Cromwell — apparently an old picture, half
length, or one third, in an oval frame — pot-
ally painted for some New-England parti-
zen. Some pictures that had been partly
obliterated by scrubbing with sand.
The dresses, embroidery, laces &c of the
Oliver family, are generally better done
than the faces. Governor Leverett's
gloves, — the gauntlet-part of leather, pretty
much modern coarse gloves, but round
the caust a stich, three or four inch
border of spangles and silver embroidery.
Old drinking glasses with tall stalks. A
black glass bottle, stamped with the
name of Philip English, with a broad
bottom. The baby-linen &c of Governor
Bradford of Plymouth province. The
club that killed old Mr. White. Old
manuscript sermons, some written
in short hand, others in a hand that
seems as if the writer had learnt to
write from print.

Nothing gives a stronger idea of old

Half a dozen, or more, family portraits of the Olivers, some in plain dresses, brown, crimson, or claret, others with gorgeous gold embroidered waistcoats, descending almost to the knees, so as to form the most conspicuous article of dress. Ladies, with lace ruffles, the painting of which, in one of the pictures, cost five guineas. Peter Oliver, who was crazy, used to fight with these family pictures, in the old mansion-house, and the face and breast of one lady bears cuts and stabs inflicted by him. Miniatures in oil, with the paint peeling off, of stern, old, yellow faces. Oliver Cromwell—apparently an old picture, half length, or one third, in an oval frame—probably painted for some New-England partisan. Some pictures that had been partly obliterated by scrubbing with sand. The dresses, embroidery, laces &c of the Oliver family, are generally better done than the faces. Governor Leverett's gloves,—the glove part of leather, pretty much modern coarse gloves, but round the wrist a deep, three or four inch border of spangles and silver embroidery— Old drinking glasses with tall stalks. A black glass bottle, stamped with the name of Philip English, with a broad bottom. The baby-linen &c of Governor Bradford of Plymouth province. The club that killed old Jo. White. Old manuscript sermons, some written in short-hand, others in a hand that seems as if the writer had learnt to write from print.

Nothing gives a stronger idea of old

worm-eaten aristocracy, of a family being weary with age, and its being time that it was extinct, then these black, dusty, faded, antique-dressed portraits, such as those of the Oliver family. — The identical old white wig of an ancient minister. — producing to us. When the impression that his very scalp, or some other portion of his personal self, would.

The excruciating agonies which Nature inflicts on men, to be represented as the work of human tormentors; — as the gout, by screwing the toes &c. Thus one might find that more than the tortures of the Romish Inquisition are daily suffered among us, without exciting notice.

Supposing a married couple fondly attached to one another, and to think that they lived solely for one another; then it to be found out that they were divorced, or that they might separate if they chose. What would be its effect?

October 7th, 1837. A walk in Northfields in the afternoon. Bright sunshine, and autumnal warmth, giving a sensation quite unlike the same degree of warmth in summer. Trees — oak, some brown, some reddish, some still green; walnuts, yellow. Fallen leaves and acorns lying beneath; the footsteps crumple in walking. In sunny spots beneath the trees, where green grass is overstrewn by the dry fallen leaves, as I passed I disturbed multitudes of

worm-eaten aristocracy, of a family's being crazy with age, and its being time that it was extinct, than these black, dusty, faded, antique-dressed portraits, such as those of the Oliver family. The identical old white wig of an ancient minister—producing somewhat the impression that his very scalp, or some other portion of his personal self, would.

The excruciating agonies which Nature inflicts on men, to be represented as the work of human tormentors;— as the gout, by screwing the toes &c. Thus we might find that [more] than the tortures of the Spanish Inquisition are daily suffered among us, without exciting notice.

Supposing a married couple fondly attached to one another, and to think that they lived solely for one another; then it to be found out that they were divorced, or that they might separate if they chose. What would be its effect?

October 7th. 1837.

A walk in Northfields in the afternoon. Bright sunshine, and autumnal warmth, giving a sensation quite unlike the same degree of warmth in summer. Trees—oak, some brown, some reddish, some still green; Walnuts yellow. Fallen leaves and acorns lying beneath; the footsteps crumple in walking. In sunny spots beneath the trees, where green grass is overstrewn by the dry fallen leaves, as I passed I disturbed multitudes of

grasshoppers, basking in the warm sunshine; and they began to hop, hop, hop,
pattering on the dry leaves like big
and heavy drops of a thunder shower.
They were invisible till they hobbled. Bees
gathering walnuts. Passed an orchard,
where two men were gathering the apples.
A wagon, with barrels stood among the
trees; the men's coats flung on the fence;
the apples lay in heaps; and each of the
men were up in a separate tree. They conversed together in loud voices, which the
air caused to ring still louder, jeering
each other, boasting of their own feats
in shaking down the apples. One got into
the very top of the tree, and gave a long
and mighty shake, and the big apples
came down, thump, thump, thump—fifty
thump, bushels hitting on the ground at
once. "There!—did you ever hear anything like that?" cried he. This nursery
scene was pretty. A horse feeding apart,
belonging to their wagon. The barberry
bushes have been red-berries on them,
but they are frost-bitten. The rose-bushes
have their scarlet seeds.

    Distant clumps of trees, now that
the variegated foliage adorns them,
have a phantasmagoria, an apparition-
like appearance. They seem to be of
some kindred to the crimson and gold
cloud-islands. It would not be strange
to see phantoms peeping forth from their
recesses. When the sun was almost below the horizon, his rays, gilding the—

grasshoppers, basking in the warm sunshine; and they began to hop, hop, hop, pattering on the dry leaves like big and heavy drops of a thunder shower. They were invisible till they hopped. Boys gathering walnuts. Passed an orchard, where two men were gathering the apples. A wagon, with barrels stood among the trees; the men's coats flung on the fence; the apples lay in heaps; and each of the men was up in a separate tree. They conversed together in loud voices, which the air caused to ring still louder, jeering each other, boasting of their own feats in shaking down the apples; one got into the very top of the tree, and gave a long and mighty shake, and the big apples came down, thump, thump, thumpetty thump, bushels hitting on the ground at once. 'There!—did you ever hear anything like that?' cried he. This sunny scene was pretty. A horse feeding apart, belonging to their wagon. The barberry bushes have some red-berries on them, but they are frost-bitten. The rose-bushes have their scarlet [pips].

Distant clumps of trees, now that the variegated foliage adorns them, have a phantasmagorian, an apparition-like appearance. They seem to be of some kindred to the crimson and gold cloud-islands. It would not be strange to see phantoms peeping forth from their recesses. When the sun was almost below the horizon, his rays, gilding the

... branches of a yellow walnut tree, had an airy and beautiful effect — the gentle contrast between the bright tufts of the yellow in the shade, and the ethereal gold in the fading sunshine. The woods that crowned distant uplands were seen to great advantage in these last rays; for the sunshine perfectly marked out and distinguished every shade of color, varnishing them as it were; while the country round, with hill and plain, being in gloomy shadow, the woods looked brighter for it.

The tide being high, had flowed almost into the cold spring, so its little current hardly issued forth from the basin. As I approached, two little eels, about as long as my finger, and slender in proportion, wriggled out of the basin; they had come from the salt water. An Indian corn field, as yet unharvested, but large and white huge golden pumpkins scattered among the hills of corn — a noble looking fruit. After the sun was down, the sky was deeply dyed with a broad sweep of gold, high towards the zenith; not flaming brightly, but somewhat dusky gold. A piece of water, extending towards the west between high banks, caught the reflection, and appeared like a sheet of brighter and more glistening gold than the sky which made it bright.

Dandelions and blue flowers are still growing in sunny places. I am in a barn a prodigious treasure of onions in their silvery coats exhaling a penetrating perfume.

upper branches of a yellow walnut tree, had an airy and beautiful
effect—the gentler contrast between the brightness of the yellow in
the shade, and the ethereal gold in the fading sunshine. The woods
that crowned distant uplands were seen to great advantage in these last
rays, for the sunshine perfectly marked out and distinguished every
shade of color, varnishing them as it were; while, the country round,
both hill and plain, being in gloomy shadow, the woods looked
brighter for it.

The tide being high, had flowed almost into the cold spring, so its
little current hardly issued forth from the basin. As I approached, two
little eels, about as long as my finger, and slender in proportion,
wriggled out of the basin; they had come from the salt water. An
Indian corn field, as yet unharvested, but dry and white. Huge golden
pumpkins scattered among the hills of corn—a noble looking fruit.
After the sun was down, they [*Hawthorne appears either to have written
"they" here—a mental lapse—or to have crossed out the beginning of another
letter after "the." The "y," if he wrote "they," is not formed in his way.*]
sky was deeply dyed with a broad sweep of gold, high towards the
zenith; not flaming brightly, but somewhat dusky gold. A piece of
water, extending towards the west between high banks, caught the
reflection, and appeared like a sheet of brighter and more
glistening-gold than the sky which made it bright.

Dandelions and blue flowers are still growing in sunny places.
Saw in a barn a prodigious treasure of onions in their silvery coats,
exhaling a penetrating perfume.

glow exceeding bright looks—the sunshine, actually reflected from a looking-
glass into a gloomy region of the chamber—
distinctly marking out the figures and colors of the paper-hangings, which are scarcely
seen elsewhere. It is like the light of mind
thrown on an obscure subject.

Man's finest workmanship, the closer
you observe it, the more imperfections it
shows:—as, on a piece of polished steel, a microscope will discover a rough surface.—
Whereas, what may look coarse and rough
in Nature's workmanship, will show an infinitely minute perfection, the closer
you look into it.

Standing in the wood-road that leads
by the Mineral Spring, and looking toward
an opposite shore of the lake, an ascending
bank with a dense border of trees, green,
yellow, red, russet, all bright colors, brightened by the mild brilliancy of the declining sun; strange to recognize the sober
old friends of Spring and Summer in this
new dress. By the bye, a pretty riddle or fable might be made out of the changes in
apparel of the familiar trees round a
house—adapted for children. But on
the lake beneath this aforesaid border
of trees—the water being not ribbled, but
its glassy surface somewhat moved and
shaken, by the remote agitation of a
breeze that was breathing on the outer
lake, this being a sort of bay—in

How exceeding bright looks the sunshine, casually reflected from a looking-glass into a gloomy region of the chamber—distinctly marking out the figure and colors of the paper-hangings, which are scarcely seen elsewhere. It is like the light of mind thrown on an obscure subject.

Man's finest workmanship, the closer you observe it, the more imperfections it shows:— as, in a piece of polished steel, a microscope will discover a rough surface.— Whereas, what may look coarse and rough in Nature's workmanship, will show an infinitely minute perfection, the closer you look into it.

Standing in the cross road that leads by the Mineral Spring, and looking towards an opposite shore of the lake, an ascending bank, with a dense border of trees, green, yellow, red, russet, all bright colors, brightened by the mild brilliancy of the declining sun; strange to recognize the sober old friends of spring and summer in this new dress. By the by, a pretty riddle or fable might be made out of the changes in apparel of the familiar trees round a house—adapted for children. But in the lake beneath this aforesaid border of trees—the water being not rippled, but its glassy surface somewhat moved and shaken, by the remote agitation of a breeze that was breathing on the outer lake, this being in a sort of bay—in the lightly agitated mirror, the variegated trees were reflected, but dreamily and indistinctly; a broad belt of bright and diversified colors were seen shining in the water beneath. Sometimes the image of a tree might be almost traced; then nothing but this sweep of broken rainbow. It was like the recollection of the real scene in an observer's mind—a confused brightness.

The reason of the minute superiority in Nature's workmanship over man's, is, that the former works from the innermost germ, while the latter works merely; superficially.

A whirlwind whirling the dried leaves round in a circle, not very violently.

To well consider the characters of a family of persons in a certain condition—poverty, for instance—and endeavor to judge how an altered condition would affect the character of each.

The aromatic smell of peat-smoke in the sunny autumnal air—very pleasant.

A walk through Beverly to Brown's hill, and home by the iron factory &c. A bright, cool afternoon. The trees, in a large part of the space through which I passed, appeared to be in their fullest glory, bright red, yellow, some of a tender green, appearing at a distance as if bedecked with new foliage, though it was likewise the effect of frost. In some places, large tracts of ground were covered as with a scarlet cloth—the underbrush being thus colored. The gen-the slightly agitated mirror, the variegated trees were reflected, but dreamily and indistinctly; a broad belt of bright and diversified colors was seen shining in the water beneath. Sometimes the image of a tree might be almost traced; then nothing but this sweep of broken rainbow. It was like the recollection of the real scene in an observers mind—a confused brightness

The reason of the minute superiority in Nature's workmanship over man's, is, that the former works from the innermost germ, while the latter works merely superficially.

A whirlwind whirling the dried leaves round in a circle, not very violently.

To well consider the characters of a family of persons in a certain condition—poverty, for instance—and endeavor to judge how an altered condition would affect the character of each.

The aromatic smell of peat-smoke in the sunny autumnal air— very pleasant

A walk through Beverley to Brown's hill, and home by the Iron factory Rd. A bright, cool afternoon. The trees, in a large part of the space through which I passed, appeared to be in their fullest glory, bright red, yellow, some of a tender green, appearing at a distance as if bedecked with new foliage, though it was likewise the effect of frost. In some places, large tracts of ground were covered as with a scarlet cloth—the underbrush being thus colored. The gen-

…real character of these autumnal colors is not gaudy, scarcely gay; there is something too deep and rich in it — it is gorgeous and magnificent, but with a sobriety diffused. The pastures at the foot of Brown's Hill were plentifully covered with barberry bushes, the leaves of which were reddish, and they were hung with prodigious quantities of berries. From the summit of the hill, looking down on tract of woodland, at a considerable distance, so that the interstices between the trees could not be seen, but that their tops presented an unbroken level, it seemed somewhat like a richly variegated carpet. The prospect from this hill is wide and interesting; but methinks it is pleasantest in the more immediate vicinity of the hill, than miles at a distance. It is pleasant to look down at the square patches of cornfields, or of potatoe grounds, of cabbages still green, or of beets looking red — all in masses, farm, in short, each portion of which he considers separately so important, while you take in the whole at a glance. Then to cast your eye over so many different establishments at once, and rapidly compare them among themselves — here a house of gentility with shady old yellow leaved elms hanging around it; then a new little white dwelling; then an old farm house; — to see the barns and sheds, and all the outhouses, clustered together; — to comprehend the oldness and…

eral character of these autumnal colors is not gaudy, scarcely gay; there is something too deep and rich in it—it is gorgeous and magnificent, but with a sobriety diffused. The pastures at the foot of Brown's Hill were plentifully covered with barberry-bushes, the leaves of which were reddish, and they were hung with prodigious quantities of berries. From the summit of the hill, looking down on tracts of woodland, at a considerable distance, so that the interstices between the trees could not be seen, but that their tops presented an unbroken level, it seemed somewhat like a richly variegated carpet. The prospect from this hill is wide and interesting; but methinks it is pleasantest in the more immediate vicinity of the hill, than miles at a distance. It is pleasant to look down at the square patches of corn fields, or of potatoe-ground, or of cabbages still green, or of beets looking red—all a mans farm, in short, each portion of which he considers separately so important, while you take in the whole at a glance. Then to cast your eye over so many different establishments at once, and rapidly compare them among themselves—here a house of gentility with shady old yellow leaved elms hanging around it; there a new little white dwelling; there an old-farm house;— to see the barns and sheds, and all the outhouses, clustered together;— to comprehend the oneness, and

& electricness, and what constitute the peculiarity of each of so many establishments, and to have in your mind a multitude of such establishments, each of which is the most important point of the world to those who live there — this really enlarges the mind, and you come down the hill much wiser than you go up. Pleasant to look over an orchard far below, and see the trees each casting its own shadow, the white spires of meeting houses, A sheet of water, partly seen among swelling lands, This Brown's Hill is a long ridge, lying at the end of a large level plain; it looks at a distance somewhat like a whale, with its head and tail under water, but its immense back protruding, with steep sides and a gradual curve along its length. When you have climbed it on one side, and gone from the summit at the other, you feel as if you had made a discovery — the landscape being quite different on the two sides. The cellar of the house, which formerly crowned the hill to be named Brown Folly, still remains, two grass grown and shallow hollows, on the highest part of the ridge. The house consisted of two wings, each perhaps sixty feet in length, united by a middle part, in which was the entrance hall, and which looked lengthwise along the hill. The foundation of a spacious porch may be traced on either side of the central portion; none of the rocks still remain, but even where they are gone, the line of the porch is still traceable by the greener verdure. In the cellar,

exclusiveness, and what constitutes the peculiarity, of each of so many establishments,—and to have in your mind a multitude of such establishments, each of which is the most important part of the world to those who live there—this really enlarges the mind, and you come down the hill somewhat wiser than you go up. Pleasant to look over an orchard far below; and see the trees each casting its own shadow. The white spires of meeting houses. A sheet of water, partly seen among swelling lands. This Brown's Hill is a long ridge, lying in the midst of a large level plain; it looks at a distance somewhat like a whale, with its head and tail under water, but its immense back protruding, with steep sides, and a gradual curve along its length. When you have climbed it one side, and gaze from the summit at the other, you feel as if you had made a discovery—the landscape being quite different on the two sides. The cellar of the house, which formerly crowned the hill to be named Brown's Folly, still remains, two grass grown and shallow hollows, on the highest part of the ridge. The house consisted of two wings, each perhaps sixty feet in length, united by a middle part, in which was the entrance-hall, and which looked lengthwise along the hill. The foundation of a spacious porch may be traced on either side of the central portion; some of the rocks still remain, but even where they are gone, the line of the porch is still traceable by the greener verdure. In the cellar, or rather the two or three, grew one or two bushels of less here, with frost-bitten berries,—there were also yarrow with its white flower, and yellow dandelion. The cellar was still deep enough to shelter a person, all but his head at least, from the wind on the summit of the hill;—but all grass grown. A line of trees seems to have been planted along the ridge of the hill. The edifice must have made quite a magnificent appearance.

Characteristics during the walk—apple trees, with only here and there an apple on the boughs, among the thinner leaves—the relics of a gathering. In others you hear a rustling, and see the boughs shaking, and hear the apples thumping down, without seeing the person who does it. Apples scattered by the wayside, some with pieces bitten out, others entire, which you pick up and taste, but find them harsh, crabbed, cider apples, though they have a pretty waxen appearance. In sunny spots of wood-land, boys in search of nuts, looking picturesque among the scarlet and golden foliage. There is something in this sunny autumnal atmosphere, that gives a peculiar effect to laughter and joyous voices—it makes them infinitely more elastic and gladsome than at other seasons. Heaps of dry leaves, tossed together by the wind, as if for a couch and lounging-place for the weary traveller, while the sun is warming it for him. Golden pumpkins and squashes, heaped in the angle of a house, till they

or rather the two cellars, grow one or two barberry bushes, with frost-bitten berries; there was also yarrow with its white flower, and yellow dandelions. The cellars were still deep enough to shelter a person, all but his head at least, from the wind on the summit of the hill;— but all grass grown. A line of trees appears to have been planted along the ridge of the hill. The edifice must have made quite a magnificent appearance.

Characteristics during the walk—apple trees, with only here and there an apple on the boughs, among the thinned leaves—the relics of a gathering. In others you hear a rustling, and see the boughs shaking, and hear the apples thumping down, without seeing the person who does it. Apples scattered by the wayside, some with pieces bitten out, others entire, which you pick up and taste, but find them harsh, crabbed, cider apples, though they have a pretty waxen appearance. In sunny spots of woodland, boys in search of nuts, looking picturesque among the scarlet and golden foliage. There is something in this sunny autumnal atmosphere, that gives a peculiar effect to laughter and joyous voices—it makes them infinitely more elastic and gladsome than at other seasons. Heaps of dry leaves, tossed together by the wind, as if for a couch and lounging-place for the weary traveller, while the sun is warming it for him. Golden pumpkins and squashes, heaped in the angle of a house, till they reach the lower windows. By teams, laden with a rustling load of Indian corn, in the bulk and ear. When an inlet of the sea runs far up into the country & you have to see a large schooner, stumpily amid the small landscape, that is unloading a cargo of wood, moist with rain, or salt water that has dashed over it. Perhaps even hear the sound of an axe in the woodland, occasionally the report of a fowling-piece. The travellers in the early part of the afternoon, look warm and comfortable, as if taking a reminiscence; but as eve draws nearer, you meet them well wrapped in surtout, or cloak, or rough great coat, and all moved within, seeming to take no great comfort in the ride, but pressing homeward. The characteristic conversation, among teamsters and country squires &c. where the ascent of a hill affords a chance to jog at the same pace as an ox-team— perhaps discussing the qualities of a yoke of oxen. The cold, bleak aspect of sheets of water. Some of the country houses with their doors closed; others still have them open, as in summer. I meet a wood-sawyer with his horse and saw on his shoulders, returning from work, as night draws on, you begin to see the gleaming of fires from the hearth on the ceilings, in the houses which you pass. Some ruddier from the chimneys. The comfortless appearance of houses at bleak and bare spots— you wonder how there can be any enjoyment in them. I meet a girl in a chintz gown, with a small shawl on her shoulders, white stockings, and summer morocco shoes— it looks observable. October 16th 1837

reach the lower windows. Ox teams, laden with a rustling load of Indian corn, in the stalk and ear. When an inlet of the sea runs far up into the country, you stare to see a large schooner, strangely amid the rural landscape; she is unloading a cargo of wood, moist with rain, or salt water that has dashed over it. Perhaps you hear the sound of an axe in the woodland. Occasionally the report of a fowling-piece. The travellers, in the early part of the afternoon, look warm and comfortable, as if taking a summer ride; but as eve draws nearer, you meet them well wrapped in surtout, or cloak, or rough greatcoat, and red-nosed withal, seeming to take no great comfort in the ride, but pressing homeward. The characteristic conversation, among teamsters and country squires &c. where the ascent of a hill compels a chaise to go at the same pace as an ox-team—perhaps discussing the qualities of a yoke of oxen. The cold, blue aspect of sheets of water. Some of the country stores with their doors closed; others still have them open, as in summer. I meet a wood-sawyer, with his horse and saw on his shoulders, returning from work. As night draws on, you begin to see the gleaming of fires from the hearth on the cielings, in the houses which you pass. Some bellies from the chimneys. The comfortless appearance of houses at bleak and bare spots—you wonder how there can be any enjoyment there. Meet a girl in a chintz gown, with a small shawl on her shoulders, white stockings, and summer morocco shoes:—it looks observable. October 14th. 1837

Turkies, queer solemn objects in black attire, grazing about, and trying to eat the fallen apples, which slip away from their mouths.

Weight, August 4, 1837. — 158 pounds.

October 16th. 1837. Spent the whole afternoon in a ramble to the sea. shore near Phillips' beach. A beautiful, sunny warm afternoon, — the very pleasantest day, probably, that there has been in the whole course of the year. People at work harvesting, without their coats. Cocks, with their squad of hens, in the grass fields, hunting grasshoppers — chasing them eagerly with out-stretched wings; appearing to take much interest in the sport, apart from the profit of it. Other hens picking at the ears of Indian corn. Grasshoppers, flies, and flying insects of all sorts, are more abundant in these warm autumnal days, than I have seen them at any other time. Yet low leather fins flutter about in the sunshine, singly, say fairs, or more, and are wafted on the gentle gales. The crickets begin to ring early in the afternoon, and sometimes a locust may be heard. In some even spots, a pleasant buzz of many insects.

Crossed the fields near Brookhouse' house, and came upon a long beach — at least a mile long, I should think — terminated by craggy rocks at either end, and backed by a high broken bank, the grassy summit of which, year by year, is continually breaking away, and precipitates to the bottom. At the foot of the bank, in some part, is a vast number of pebbles and large stones. rolled up

Turkies, queer solemn objects in black attire, grazing about, and trying to eat the fallen apples, which slips away from their mouths.

Weight, August, 1837.— 158 pounds.

October 16th. 1837. [*Hawthorne started to write "17," changed to "16th"*]

Spent the whole afternoon in a ramble to the sea-shore near Phillips' beach. A beautiful, sunny warm afternoon,—the very pleasantest day, probably, that there has been in the whole course of the year. People at work harvesting, without their coats. Cocks, with their squad of hens, in the grass fields, hunting grashoppers—chasing them eagerly with outstretched wings, appearing to take much interest in the sport, apart from the profit. Other hens picking at the ears of Indian corn. Grashoppers, flys, and flying insects of all sorts, are more abundant in these warm autumnal days, than I have seen them at any other time. Yellow butterflies flutter about in the sunshine, singly, by pairs, or more, and are wafted on the gentle gales. The crickets begin to sing early in the afternoon, and sometimes a locust may be heard. In some warm spots, a pleasant buzz of many insects.

Crossed the fields near Brookhouse's house, and came upon a long beach—at least a mile long, I should think—terminated by craggy rocks at either end, and backed by a high broken bank, the grassy summit of which, year by year, is continually breaking away and precipitated to the bottom. At the foot of the bank, in some parts, is a vast number of pebbles and paving stones, rolled up

thither by the sea long ago. The beach
is of a brown sand, or with hardly any pebbles intermixed upon it. When the tide
is part way down, there is a margin of
several yards from the water's edge,
along the whole mile length of the beach,
which glistens like a mirror, and reflects
objects, and shines bright in the sunshine—
the sand being wet to that distance from
the water. Above this margin, the sand
is not wet, and grows less and less damp
the farther towards the bank you keep.
In some places, your footstep is perfectly
implanted, showing the whole shape, and
the square toe, and every nail in the heel of
your boot. Elsewhere the impression is imperfect, and even when you stamp, you do
not imprint the whole. As you tread, a
dry spot flashes around your footstep,
and grows moist as you lift your foot
again. Pleasant to pace along this often-
dris walk, watching the surf-wave, how
sometimes it seems to make a feint of
breaking, but dies away ineffectually,
merely kissing the strand; then, after many
such abortive efforts, it gathers itself, and
forms a high wall, and rolls onward, heightened
being and heightened &, without foam or the
movement of the green line, and at last
throws itself fiercely on the beach, with
a loud roar, the spray flying above. As
you walk along, you are preceded by a
flock of twenty or thirty beach birds, which
are seeking, I suppose, for food among the cav-
ities of the surf, yet seem to be merely
sporting, chasing the sea as it retires, and
running up before the impending wave. Some-
they let it come there off their feet, and
float lightly on its breaking summit; sometimes they flutter and seem to rest on the

thither by the sea long ago. The beach is of a brown sand, with hardly
any pebbles intermixed upon it. When the tide is part way down,
there is a margin of several yards from the water's edge, along the
whole mile length of the beach, which glistens like a mirror, and
reflects objects, and shines bright in the sunshine—the sand being wet
to that distance from the water. Above this margin, the sand is not
wet, and grows less and less damp the further towards the bank you
keep. In some places, your footstep is perfectly-implanted, showing
the whole shape, and the square toe, and every nail in the heel of
your boot. Elsewhere the impression is imperfect, and even when you
stamp, you do not imprint the whole. As you tread, a dry spot flashes
around your footstep, and grows moist as you lift your foot again.
Pleasant to pace along this extensive walk, watching the surf-wave,
how sometimes it seems to make a feint of breaking, but dies away
ineffectually, merely kissing the strand; then, after many such abortive
efforts, it gathers itself, and forms a high wall, and rolls onward
heightening and heightening, without foam at the summit of the green
line, and at last throws itself fiercely on the beach, with a loud roar,
the spray flying above. As you walk along, you are preceded by a
flock of twenty or thirty beach birds, which are seeking, I suppose, for
food on the margin of of the surf, yet seem to be merely sporting,
chasing the sea as it retires, and running up before the impending
wave. Some- they let it bear them off their feet, and float lightly on its
breaking summit; sometimes they flutter and seem to rest on the

feathery spray. They are little birds with gray backs and snow white bellies; their image may be seen in the wet margin, almost or quite as distinctly as the reality. Their legs are long. As you draw near, they take flight of a score of yards or more, and then recommence their dalliance with the surf-wave. You may behold their unutterable now little tracks in the wet sand. Before you reach the end of the beach, you become quite attached to these little sea-birds, and take much interest in their occupations. After passing the length of the beach, pleasant there to turn back and retrace your footsteps, your tracks being all traceable, you may recall the whole mood and occupation of your mind during your first passage. Here again turned down. What aside, to pick up a shell that you saw near the water's edge. Here you accumulated a long sea weed, and trailed it at length after you for a considerable dis-tance. Here you fronted the sea, looking at a sail, distant in the sunny blue; here you looked at some shells on the bank. Here your vagary of mind seems to have bewildered you; for your tracks go round round, and interchange each other, without visible reason. Here you brushed up pebbles and skipped them upon the water. Here you wrote names and made figures with a razor sea-shell, in the sand.

After leaving the beach, I clambered over rocks, all shattered and tossed about every how; in some parts curiously worn and hollowed out, almost into caverns, by the sea. The rocks, shagged with sea

feathery spray. They are little birds with gray backs and snow white bellies; their images may be seen in the wet margin, almost or quite as distinctly as the reality. Their legs are long. As you draw near, they a flight of a score of yards or more, and then recommence their dalliance with the surf-wave. You may behold their multitudinous little tracks in the wet sand. Before you reach the end of the beach, you become quite attached to these little sea-birds, and take much interest in their occupations. After pacing the length of the beach, pleasant then to turn back and retrace your footsteps. Your tracks being all traceable, you may recall the whole mood and occupation of your mind during your first passage. Here you turned somewhat aside, to pick up a shell that you saw nearer the water's edge. Here you examined a long sea weed, and trailed its length after you for a considerable distance. /Here the aspect of the wide deep struck you suddenly—/ Here you fronted the sea, looking at a sail, distant in the sunny blue; here you looked at some plant on the bank. Here some vagary of mind seems to have bewildered you; for your tracks go round round, and interchange each other, without visible reason. /A horse-shoe/ Here you picked up pebbles and skipped them upon the water. Here you wrote names and made faces with a razor sea-shell, in the sand.

After leaving the beach, clambered over crags, all shattered and tossed about, every how; in some parts curiously worn and hollowed out, almost into caverns, by the sea. The rock, shagged with sea

weird. In some places, a thick carpet of sea
weed laid over the pebbles, into which your
foot would sink. Deep tanks among these
rocks, which the sea replenishes at high
tide, and then leaves, the bottom all covered
with various sorts of sea-plants, as if it
were some sea-monster's private garden.
I saw a crab in one of them; five-fingers
too. From the edge of the rocks, you can
very look off into deep, dark water, even
at low tide. Among the rocks, I found
a dead bird — whether a wild goose, a
loon, or an albatross, I scarcely know. It
was in such a position that I almost fancied it might be asleep, and therefore
drew near softly, lest it should take
flight; but it was dead, and stirred
not when I touched it. Sometimes a dead
body is cast up. A ledge of rocks with a beacon on it, looking like a monument erected
to those who have perished by shipwreck.
The smoke of a stampore fire-place, where a
party have cooked their fish.

　　About midway on the beach, a fresh-
water brooklet flows towards the sea.
Where it leaves the land, it is quite a re-
pulsing little current, but in flowing across
the sand, it grows shallower and more
shallow, and at last is quite lost, and
dies in the effort to carry its little tribute
to the main.

　　An article to be made of telling the thoughts
of the tiles of an old-fashioned chimney-piece,
to a child.

　　A person conscious that he was soon
to die, the manner in which he would pay his
last visit to familiar persons and things.

　　A description of the various classes of hotels
and taverns, and the prominent personages in
each. There should be some story

weed. In some places, a thick carpet of sea weed laid over the pebbles, into which your foot would sink. Deep tanks among these rocks, which the sea replenishes at high tide and then leaves, the bottom all covered with various sorts of sea-plants, as if it were some sea-monsters private garden. I saw a crab in one of them; five-fingers too. From the edge of the rocks, you may look off into deep, deep water, even at low tide. Among the rocks, I found a great bird— whether a wild goose, a loon, or an albatross, I scarcely know. It was in such a position that I almost fancied it might be asleep, and therefore drew near softly, lest it should take flight; but it was dead, and stirred not when I touched it. Sometimes a dead fish cast up. A ledge of rocks with a beacon it, looking like a monument erected to those who have perished by shipwreck. The smoked extempore fire-place, where a party have cooked their fish.

About midway on the beach, a fresh-water brooklet flows towards the sea. Where it leaves the land, it is quite a rippling little current, but in flowing across the sand, it grows shallower and more shallow, and at last is quite lost and dies in the effort to carry its little tribute to the main

An article to be made of telling the stories of the tiles of an old-fashioned chimney piece, to a child.

A person conscious that he was soon to die, the humor in which he would pay his last visit to familiar persons and things.

A description of the various classes of hotels and taverns, and the prominent personages in each. There should be some story

connected with it — as of a person commencing with boarding at a great Hotel, and
gradually, as his means grew less, descending
in life, till he got below ground, into a cellar.

Scene in the Capitol — Rule as a receptacle
of Indian chiefs — the lobby of the House &c — a Sy-
ces of articles.

A person to see in the profession of some thing
as perfect as mortal man has a right to demand; he tries to make it better, and ruins
it entirely: — For instance, a noble mansion,
and in his attempt to improve it, he causes
it to fall to the ground.

A person to spend all his life and splendid talents in trying to achieve some thing naturally impossible — as to make a conquest over
nature —

Meditation about the main gas pipe of
a great city — if the supply were to be
stopped, what would happen. How many
different scenes it sheds light on. It might
be made emblematical of some thing.

Dec. 6th. 1837. Mild weather. Streaks
of snow herecall the storm weekly; and beds
of snow in the hollows of hills. The grass
still green and living in some places; and leaves
of clover. Cows grazing along the roadside, but picking up little.

A fairy-tale about chasing Echo to her
hiding place. Echo a the voice of a reflection in a mirror.
"Love" wisely, but not too well."

connected with it—as of a person commencing with boarding at a great hotel, and gradually, as his means grew less, descending in life, till he got below ground, into a cellar.

Service in the Capitol—such as a reception of Indian chiefs—the Lobby of the House &c.— a series of articles.

A person to be in the possession of something as perfect as mortal man has a right to demand; he tries to make it better, and ruins it entirely:— For instance, a noble mansion, and in his attempts to improve it, he causes it to fall to the ground.

A person to spend all his life and splendid talents in trying to achieve something naturally impossible—as to make a conquest over nature—[*1 3/4 lines inked out*]

Meditations about the main gas pipe of a great city—if the supply were to be stopped, what would happen. How many different scenes it sheds light on. It might be made emblematical of something.

Decr. 6th. 1837. [*Hawthorne started to write "Nov.," changed to "Decr."*]

Mild weather. Streaks of snow beneath the stone walls; and spots of snow in the hollows of hills. The grass still green and living in some places; and leaves of clover. Cows grazing along the roadside, but picking up little.

A fairy-tale about chasing Echo to her hiding-place. Echo is the voice of a reflection in a mirror.

'Love "wisely, but not too well."

A house to be built over a natural Spring of inflammable gas, and to be constantly illuminated therewith. What moral could be drawn from this? It is carburetted hydrogen gas, and is evolved from a soft shale or slate, which is sometimes bituminous, and contains more or less carbonate of lime. It appears in the vicinity of Lockport and Niagara Falls, and elsewhere in New-York. I believe it indicates coal. At Fredonia, the whole village is lighted by it. Elsewhere, a farm-house was lighted by it; and no other fuel used in the coldest weather.

Gnomes, or other mischievous little fiends, to be represented as burrowing in the hollow teeth of some person who had subjected himself to their power. It should be a child's story. This should be one of many modes of petty torment. They should be contrasted with beneficent fairies, who minister to the pleasures of the good.

A man will undergo great toil and hardship for ends that must be many years distant — as wealth or fame — but none for an end that may be close at hand; as the joys of Heaven.

A company of men, none of whom have anything worth hoping for on earth, yet who do not look forward to anything beyond earth.

Sorrow to be personified, and its effect on a family represented, by the way in which the members of the family regard this dark-clad and sad-browed inmate.

A story to show how an all envelopes and wrongs, and avenge one another; as a man is jilted by a rich girl, and jilts a poor one.

A house to be built over a natural spring of inflammable gas, and to be constantly illuminated therewith. What moral could be drawn from this? It is carburetted hydrogen gas, and is evolved from a soft shale or slate, which is sometimes butuminous and contains more or less carbonate of lime. It appears in the vicinity of Lockport and Niagara Falls, and elsewhere in New-York. I believe it indicates coal. At Fredonia, the whole village is lighted by it. Elsewhere, a farm-house was lighted by it, and no other fuel used in the coldest weather.

Gnomes, or other mischievous little fiends, to be represented as burrowing in the hollow teeth of some person who had subjected himself to their power. It should be a child's story. This should be one of many modes of petty torment. They should be contrasted with beneficent fairies, who minister to the pleasures of the good.

A man will undergo great toil and hardship for ends that must be many years distant—as wealth or fame—but none for an end that may be close at hand; as the joys of Heaven.

A company of men, none of whom have any thing worth hoping for on earth, yet who do not look forward to anything beyond earth.

Sorrow to be personified, and its effect on a family represented, by the way in which the members of the family regard this dark-clad and sad-browed inmate.

A story to show how we are all wronged and wrongers, and avenge one another; as a man is jilted by a rich girl, and jilts a poor one.

To personify winds of various characters.

A man living a wicked life in one place, and simultaneously, a virtuous and religious one in another.

An ornament to be worn upon the person of a lady — or a jewelled heart. After many years, it happens to be broken, or unscrewed, and a poisonous perfume comes out. A bottle of poison kept a long while, and supposed to be a potent medicine — or vice versa.

In love-quarrels, a man goes off on stilts, and comes back on his knees.

David Roberts.

Lieut. Frank White of the Navy [ ] an inveterate duellist, and on learning that he had taken offence with Lieut. French, now captain Bolton, and endeavored to draw him into a duel, following him to the Mediterranean for that purpose, and harrassing him intolerably. At last, both parties being in Massachusetts, French determined to fight, and applied to Lieut. Armstrong to be his second. Armstrong examined into the merits of the quarrel, and came to the conclusion that French had not given White justifiable cause for driving him to a duel, and that he ought not to be shot. He instructed French in the use of the pistol, and, before the meeting, warned him, by all

To personify winds of various characters.

A man living a wicked life in one place, and simultaneously, a virtuous and religious one in another.

An ornament to be worn upon the person of a lady—as a jewelled heart. After many years, it happens to be broken, or unscrewed, and a poisonous perfume comes out. A bottle of poison kept a long while, and supposed to be a potent medicine—<u>or vice versa</u>.

In love-quarrels a man goes off on stilts, and comes back on his knees.

David Roberts.

Lieut. Frank White of the Navy (nephew of Judge Story) was an inveterate duellist, and an unerring shot. He had taken offence with Lieut. Finch, now Captain Bolton, and endeavored to draw him into a duel, following him to the Mediterranean for that purpose, and harrassing him intolerably. At last, both parties being in Massachusetts, Finch determined to fight, and applied to Lieut. Armstrong to be his second. Armstrong examined into the merits of the quarrel, and came to the conclusion that Finch had not given White justifiable cause for driving him to a duel, and that he ought not to be shot. He instructed Finch in the use of the pistol, and, before the meeting, warned him, by all means, to get the first fire; for that if White fired first, he, French, was infallibly a dead man, as his antagonist could shoot to a hair's breadth. The parties met; and French, firing immediately on the word's being given, shot White through the heart. White, with a most savage expression of countenance, fired, after the bullet had gone through his heart, and when the blood had entirely left his face, and shot away one of French's side locks. His face probably looked as if he were already in the Hell, whither he went at the same instant. As afterwards it appeared, an angel's calmness and ichor.

Elizabeth P. Peabody's great friend with Ce. from a sudden fright, was seized with a trembling, which continued during her whole subsequent life. It was a serious affection. This idea might be made into something.

A company of persons to drink a certain medicinal preparation, and it to prove a poison or the contrary, according to their different characters.

Scene in Mr. Robert's office — Police Judge Clark proposing to Rev. Mr. Upham — to marry a couple who were waiting in his office. The fellow had seduced the girl and gone off — she having a child during his absence. On his return, he was brought before the police, and expressed his willingness to marry the girl; but it was considered dangerous to trust him at large.

means, to get the first fire; for that if White fired first, he, Finch, was infallibly a dead man, as his antagonist could shoot to a hair's breadth. The parties met; and Finch, firing immediately on the word's being given, shot White through the heart. White, with a most savage expression of countenance, fired, after the bullet had gone through his heart, and when the blood had entirely left his face, and shot away one of Finch's side locks. His face probably looked as if he were already in the Hell, whither he went at this same instant. /But afterwards it assumed an angelic calmness and repose./

Elizabeth P. Peabody's great-grand mother, from a severe fright, was seized with a trembling, which continued during her whole subsequent life. It was a nervous affection. This idea might be made into something.

A company of persons to drink a certain medicinal preparation, and it to prove a poison or the contrary, according to their different characters.

Scene in Mr. Roberts' office—Police Judge Mack proposing to Rev. Mr. Upham to marry a couple who were waiting in his office. The fellow had seduced the girl and gone off—she having a child during his absence. On his return, he was brought before the police, and expressed his willingness to marry the girl; but it was considered dangerous to trust him at large during the time requisite for publication of the banns,— the alternative, therefore, seemed to be, between marriage and committal to jail. Mr. Upham demurred against violating the marriage statutes, yet was unwilling not to lend a hand in obtaining justice for the girl and her child — which latter would be, to a certain extent, legitimated. Moreover, he seemed to consider that he should be partly responsible for the illegitimate intercourse what would doubtless continue to be carried on. After consulting of the revised statutes, Judge Meeke declined to marry them himself, because, having once before haltered a couple, the union had turned out so unhappily, that he had resolved never to burthen his conscience with such another act. Mr. Upham seemed to be more hardened in the performance of his awful duty. Finally, the couple were dismissed unmarried— the man giving the girl a note for $400, as security for marrying her. The girl appeared willing to trust to his faith, and thought it would be more decent to wait for publication. Among Mr. Upham's proposals was to give the ceremony the sanctions of religion, if Judge Meeke would perform it. I was sorry that the affair did not end in marriage.

during the time requisite for publication of the banns;— the
alternative, therefore, seemed to be, between marriage and committal
to jail. Mr. Upham demurred against violating the marriage statute;
yet was unwilling not to lend a hand in obtaining justice for the girl
and her child—which latter would be, to a certain extent, legitimated.
Moreover, he seemed to consider that he should be partly
responsible for the illegitimate intercourse which would doubtless
continue to be carried on. Much consulting of the revised statutes.
Judge Mack declined to marry them himself, because, having once
before haltered a couple, the union had turned out so unhappily, that
he had resolved never to burthen his conscience with such another
act. Mr. Upham seemed to be more hardened in the performance of
his awful duty. Finally, the couple were dismissed unmarried—the man
giving the girl a note for $400, as security for marrying her. The girl
appeared willing to trust to his faith, and thought it would be more
decent to wait for publication. Among Mr. Upham's proposals was to
give the ceremony the sanctions of religion, if Judge Mack would
perform it. I was sorry that the affair did not end in marriage.

Many persons, without consciousness of so doing, to contribute to some one end; — as a beggar's feast, made out of broken victuals from many tables; — or a public carpet, woven of threads from innumerable garments.

The Fremont supper table, between nine and eleven, o'clock — spread with cold fowl, joints of meat, ham, bread, butter &c. Water for the general drink. Roast potatoes, unpeeled. Gentlemen scattered along it, singly or by pairs. One, bald-headed, with a double bottle of porter by him — a pair drinking champagne, the cork of which, being cut by the waiter, flew up and is seen to strike the canvas ceiling; a large bottle and a small one. They laugh and are very merry, while the porter-drinkers talk seriously of matters of state &c. A large coal fire burning comfortably; the wind whistling and howling out-of-doors, — a clear night.

A dreadful secret to be communicated to many people, of various characters — grave & gay — and they all to become insane, according to their several characters, by the influence of the secret.

Some very famous jewel, or other thing, much talked of all over the world. Some person to meet with it, and get possession of it, in some unexpected manner, amid homely circumstances.

Many persons, without consciousness of so doing, to contribute to some one end;— as a beggar's feast, made up of broken victuals from many tables;— or a patch carpet, woven of shreds from innumerable garments.

The Tremont supper-table, between nine and eleven °clock— spread with cold fowl, joints of meat, ham, bread, butter &c. Water for the general drink. Roast potatoes, unpeeled. Gentlemen scattered along it, singly, or by pairs. One, perhaps, with a small bottle of porter by him—one pair drinking champagne, the cork of which, being cut by the waiter, flys up and is seen to strike the carved cieling; a large bottle and a small one. They laugh and are very merry, while the porter-drinkers talk seriously of matters of state &c. A large coal fire burning comfortably; the wind whistling and howling out of doors, in Beacon street.

A dreadful secret to be communica- to several people, of various characters—grave or gay—and they all to become insane, according to their several characters, by the influence of the secret.

Some very famous jewel, or other thing, much talked of all over the world. Some person to meet with it, and get possession of it, in some unexpected manner, amid homely circumstances.

To poison a person, or a party of persons, with the sacramental wine.

Stories to be told of a certain person's appearance in public, and been seen in various situations, and making visits in private circles: but, finally, one looking for this person, to come upon his old grave, and mossy tombstones.

A cloud in the shape of an old woman, kneeling, with arms extended towards the moon &c—

Dolorita, daughter of Feliciana — grief, the daughter of Felicity.

Don Manuel was piernas longas of floreas

Tie a piece of sewing-silk to a great silver-tongued — sounds like the bell of the cathedral of Havana — grand, tremendous sound

"Dear Mother, there is no telling how she sleeps — it would do your very heart good to go into the room and see her stretched in a calm and deep slumber, unconscious of all that may be going on, — and then waking up as if she were just awake!"
M. F. P. of Sophia

On being transported to things unseen, we feel as if all were unreal. This is but the perception of the true unreality of earthly things, made evident by the want of congruity between ourselves and them. By and bye, we become unreally adapted, and the perception is lost.

To poison a person, or a party of persons, with the sacramental wine.

Stories to be told of a certain person's appearance in public, and been seen in various situations, and making visits in private circles; but, finally, one looking for this person, to come upon his old grave, and mossy tomb-stone.

A cloud in the shape of an old woman, kneeling, with arms extended towards the moon &c.

Dolorita, daughter of Feliciana—Grief, the daughter of Felicity.

Don. Manuel con piernas longos y flaccas.

Tie a piece of sewing-silk to a great silver spoon—sounds like the bell of the cathedral of Havana—grand, tremendous sound

"Dear Mother, there is no telling how she sleeps—it would do your very heart good to go into the room and see her stretched in a calm and deep slumber, unconscious of all that may be going on,—and then waking up as if she were just made."

M. T. P. of Sophia

On being transported to strange scenes, we feel as if all were unreal. This is but the perception of the true unreality of earthly things, made evident by the want of congruity between ourselves and them. By and bye, we become mutually adapted, and the the perception is lost.

"A plain green silk open riding-dress,
lined through with stiff white satin,— &
a red embroidered India muslin underneath,
and a straw hat loaded with flowers; —
a curious gold chain, quarter of an inch broad,
round her neck, with a watch; and a diamond on her finger that illuminated the
corner where she sat." Dress of high
Spanish lady in interior of Cuba.

"It seemed exactly as if they had received sentence to dance for some crime."—
the energy, and industry, and anxiety, and
fury &c. "with which they flourished their
feet and whirled each other round."
                Cuban peasants at a ball.

"A huge woman and her three thin-lined
away at it with the greatest vengeance —
the more quizzical, because no dance is
so easy, light, and gentle as this, when
properly performed.

"A blue satin boddice laced in front
over a white satin chemisette, and a bird
of Paradise, & blue silky dress; a necklace of pearl, and pearl fillet round her
head, and pearl earrings."
                Ball dress, Cuba.

"The house "was in a whisper!" — on account of a person's being sick.

White muslin with short sleeves, Rebel set
of cornelians set in finely wrought gold — necklace, ear-rings and pins; gold chain round her
head, and pearls of cornelian on forehead Gold
colored belt and gold pocket kerchief.
                Ball dress.

"A plaid green silk open riding-dress, lined through with stiff white satin—& a rich embroidered India muslin underneath, and a straw hat loaded with flowers;— a massive gold chain, quarter of an inch broad, round her neck, with a watch; and a diamond on her finger that illuminated the corner where she sat." Dress of high Spanish lady in interior of Cuba.

"It seemed exactly as if they had received sentence to dance for some crime."—the energy, and industry, and anxiety, and frenzy &c. "with which they flourished their feet and whirled each other round."

Cuban peasants at a ball.

"A huge woman and her spouse thundered away at it with the greatest vengeance—the more quizzical, because her dance is so airy, light, and gentle as the waltz—properly performed.

"A blue satin-boddice laced in front over a white satin chemisette, and a bird of Paradise, & blue silky dress; a necklace of pearl, and pearl fillet round her head, and pearl ear-rings."

Ball dress, Cuba.

"The house was in a whisper."— on account of a person's being sick.

White muslin with short sleeves. Superb set of Cornelians set in finely wrought gold—necklace, ear-rings and pin; gold chain round her head, and jewel of cornelian on forehead. Gold colored belt and gold gauze kerchief.

Ball dress.

"Hands — who looks as if something had
once astonished him, and before the surprise
was over, his face had frozen into an expression
of everlasting wonder."

Sophia Peabody.

"Who ever ate with such a fork but Oberon."
A lady finding a dog with her fingers.
Do.

Immeasurably great. grandfather."
Do.

A bird is often calling "Sophie" in the woods —
being its highest note. A lady's head have might
be supposed to speak in the bird's own

"Ten hundred thousand mole-hills would make
a respectable mountain." S. P.

A Cleaning an obscure old picture,

Miss Taylor of New Hampshire — the perfection
of manly beauty, when young. "More than one
lady has been found dead with his miniature
tied round her neck. The miniature was copied,
and possessed by many. A great artist, please-
writer &c — and a comparison of Danaë's. One
at Peale's Museum in N.Y. he stood for a
wooden statue of Apollo. A party of girls
visiting the museum, were delighted with
the statue — one of them got over the railing
with intent to kiss it. The statue came
to life, being a living woman, and
the poor girl fainted

"Manos—who looks as if something had once astonished him, and before the surprise was over, his face had frozen into an expression of everlasting wonder."

Sophia Peabody.

"Who ever ate with such a fork but Oscar."—A lady feeding a dog with her fingers.

Do.

Immeasurably great-grandfather."

Do.

A bird in Cuba calling "Sophie" in the woods—being its single note. A lady's dead lover might be supposed to speak in the bird's voice

"Ten hundred thousand mole-hills would make a respectable mountain." S. P.

Cleaning an obscure old picture.

Judge Tyler of New Hampshire—the perfection of manly beauty, when young. "More than one lady has been found dead, with his miniature round her neck. The miniature was copied and possessed by many. A great wit, play-writer &c—and a companion of Dennie. Once at Pearle's Museum in N.Y. he stood for a waxen statue of Apollo. A party of girls visiting the museum were delighted with the statue—one of them got over the railing with intent to kiss it. The statue came to life, like Pygmalion's woman, and the poor girl fainted.

An old looking-glass — Somebody finds out the secret of making all the images that have been reflected in it pass back again across its surface.

Our Indian races having reared no monuments, like the Greeks, Romans, & Egyptians, when they have disappeared from the earth, their history will be a fable, and they misty phantoms.

A woman to sympathise with all emotions, but to have none of her own.

The influence of a peculiar mind, in close communion with another, to drive the latter to insanity.

Scene in a mad-house — a gentleman suspicious of a pre-disposition to insanity, and who had once had a fit of it, watching each patient with shuddering sympathy.

To look at a beautiful girl, in her chamber or elsewhere, and picture all the lovers, in different situations, whose hearts are centered on her.

A portrait of a person in N. England to be recognised as of the same person represented by a portrait in Old England. Having distinguished himself there, he had suddenly vanished, and had never been heard of — till he was thus discovered to be identical with a distinguished man of N. England.

Nov. 15th. The red light which the Sun sets at this season diffuse, — there being thievery of tenuous — but the sun setting bright amid clouds, and diffuses if its radiance over clouds that—

An old looking-glass—somebody finds out the secret of making all the images that have been reflected in it pass back again across its surface.

Our Indian races having reared no monuments, like the Greeks, Romans, & Egyptians, when they have disappeared from the earth, their history will appear a fable, and they misty phantoms.

A woman to symphise with all emotions, but to have none of her own.

The influence of a peculiar mind, in close communion with another, to drive the latter to insanity.

Scene in a mad-house—a gentleman conscious of a pre-disposition to insanity, and who had once had a fit of it, watching each patient with shuddering sympathy.

To look at a beautiful girl, in her chamber or elsewhere, and picture all the lovers, in different situations, whose hearts are centered on her.

A portrait of a person in N. England to be recognized as of the same person represented by a portrait in Old-England. Having distinguished himself there, he had suddenly vanished, and had never been heard of—till he was thus discovered to be identical with a distinguished man of N. England.

June 15th.

The red light which the sunsets at this season diffuse;—these being showery afternoons—but the sun setting bright amid clouds, and diffusing its radiance over clouds scat-

tint in masses all over the sky. It gives
a rich tinge to all objects, even those of sombre hues, yet without changing their hues.
The complexions of people are exceedingly
enriched by it; the girls look warm and
voluptuous – not languidly voluptuous, but
with a mild fire. The whole scenery and
pasturages acquire, we thinks, a passionate character. A lover scene should be laid
on such an evening. The trees and the
grass have now the brightest possible green,
there having been so many showers alternating with real powerful sunshine. There
are roses and tulips, and honeysuckles with
their sweet smell; in short the splendor
of a more gorgeous climate than ours
ought to be brought into the picture.

The situation of a man, in the midst of a
crowd, yet as completely in the power of another,
life and all, as if they two were in the deepest
solitude.

Feb. 16. Monday. 1838. A very hot, bright.
Sunny day; town much thronged. Booths
on the common, selling gingerbread &c.: suga-
plums and confectionary, spruce-beer, lemonade. Spirits forbidden, but probably sold
stealthily. On the top of one of the booths, a
monkey, with a tail two or three feet long.
He is fastened by a cord, which getting
tangled with the flag over the booth, he takes
hold and tries to free it. The object of much
attention from the crowd, and played with
by the boys, who toss up gingerbread to him

tered in masses all over the sky. It gives a rich tinge to all objects, even those of sombre hues, yet without changing their hues; the complexions of people are exceedingly enriched by it; the girls look warm and voluptuous—not languidly voluptuous, but with a mild fire. The whole scenery and personages acquire, methinks, a passionate character. A love-scene should be laid on such an evening. The trees and the grass have now the brightest possible green, there having been so many showers alternating with such powerful sunshine. There are roses and tulips, and honeysucker with their sweet smell; in short the splendor of a more gorgeous climate than ours might be brought into the picture.

The situation of a man, in the midst of a crowd, yet as completely in the power of another, life and all, as if they two were in the deepest solitude.

Fourth July. 1838.

A very hot, bright sunny day; town much thronged. Booths on the common, selling gingerbread &c. sugar-plums and confectionery, spruce-beer, lemonade. Spirits forbidden, but probably sold stealthily. On the top of one of the booths a monkey, with a tail two or three feet long. He is fastened by a cord, which, getting tangled with the flag over the booth, he takes hold and tries to free it. The object of much attention from the crowd, and played with by the boys, who toss up ginger bread to him which he nibbles and throws down again. He reciprocates notice of some kind or other, with all who notice him. A sort of gracity about him. A boy pulls his long tail, whereat he gives a slight squeak, and for the future elevates it as much as possible. Look-ing at the same booth by and large find that the poor monkey has been obliged to be-take himself to the top of one of the wooden posts that stick up high above. — Boys going about with oranges & candy, almost sold, else will eat; — a collection of painters, unusual-ness &c in every. Smell of cigars, from gen-tlemen down to immense long canes, smoking among the crowd. Constables in considerable number parading about with their staves, some-times communing with each other, producing an effect by their presence without having to interfere actively. One or two old ladies or others rather the worse for liquor; in gen-eral people very temperate. At evening the aspect of things on the move; picturesque group down of the booth-keepers knocking away the temporary structures, and putting the materials in wagons to carry away; other booths lighted up; and the lights gleaming through rents in the ragged cloth &c. Cus-tomers rather victims, yet knowing gen'ly boldly and then really for what they want; young sailors &c: a young fellow and a girl coming arm in arm; perhaps two girls ap-proaching the booth, and getting into conversa-tion with the folks thereabout; while old knowing codgers wink to one another

which he nibbles and throws down again. He reciprocates notice of
some kind or other, with all who notice him. A sort of gravity about
him. A boy pulls his long tail, whereat he gives a slight squeak, and
for the future elevates it as much as possible. Looking at the same
booth by and bye, find that the poor monkey has been obliged to
betake him self to the top of one of the wooden joists that stick up
high above.— Boys going about with molasses candy, almost melted
down in the sun.— Shows, a mammoth rat; a collection of pirates,
murderers &c. in wax. Smell of cigars, from Spanish down to immense
long nines, smoking among the crowd. Constables in considerable
number, parading about with their staves, sometimes communing with
each other, producing an effect by their presence without having to
interfere actively. One or two old salts or others rather the worse for
liquor; in general people very temperate. At evening the aspect of
things rather more picturesque; some of the booth keepers knocking
down the temporary structures, and putting the materials in wagons to
carry away; other booths lighted up; and the lights gleaming through
rents in the sail-cloth top. Customers rather riotous, yet funny, calling
loudly and whimsically for what they want,—young sailors &c; a young
fellow and a girl coming arm in arm; perhaps two girls approaching the
booth, and getting into conversation with the he-folks thereabout,
while old knowing codgers wink to one another

thereby indicating their opinion that these ladies are of easy virtue. — Perhaps a knock-down between two half-sleeves fellows in the crowd — a knock-down — with a heavy blow, the receiver being scarcely able to keep his footing at any rate. Shoutings and hallooings, laughter — oaths — generally a good-natured tumult; and the coarse talk; use no slovenly, but in temper, if at all, in a friendly sort of way. Talk with one about how the day has spent, and bears testimony to the orderliness of the crowd, respects over booth, of selling liquor, relates an scuffle &c. — Perhaps a talkative and witty seller of gingerbread &c. holding forth to the people from his cart, making himself quite a noted character by his readiness of remark and humor; and selling off all his wares. — Late in the evening, deemed the work, people consulting how they are to get home, many having long miles to walk; a father with wife and children, saying it will be 12 o'clock before they reach home, the children being already tired to death; — girls going home with their beaux; may they not linger by the wayside. The moon being lately dim the bright not giving so white a light as sometimes; the girls all look beautiful and fairy like in it, not quite distinct, nor yet dim; the different character of female countenances as observed during the day — mirthful and mischievous, slyly humorous; stupid &c; looking genteel generally; but when they speak,

thereby indicating their opinion that these ladies are of easy virtue.—
Perchance a knock-down between two half-stewed fellows in the
crowd—a knock-down without a heavy blow, the receiver being
scarcely able to keep his footing at any rate. Shoutings and hallooings,
laughter,—oaths—generally a good-natured tumult; and the constables
use no severity, but interfere, if at all, in a friendly sort of way. Talk
with one about how the day has past, and bears testimony to the
orderliness of the crowd, suspects one booth of selling liquor, relates
one scuffle &c.— Perhaps a talkative and witty seller of gingerbread
&c, holding forth to the people from his cart, making himself quite a
noted character by his readiness of remark and humor; and selling off
all his wares.— Late in the evening, during the fire works, people
consulting how they are to get home, many having long miles to walk;
a father with wife and children, saying it will be 12 °clock before they
reach home, the children being already tired to death;— girls going
home with their beaus; may they not linger by the wayside. The moon
beautifully dark bright, not giving so white a light as sometimes. The
girls all look beautiful and fairy like in it, not exactly distinct, nor yet
dim. The different character of female countenances as observed
during the day—mirthful and mischievous, slyly humorous, stupid &c;
looking genteel generally, but when they speak,

of the betraying plebeianism by the tones of their voices — Two girls on the window very tired — on a pale, thin, languid looking creature; the other plump, rosy, rather overburdened with her own little body. Conversation of the various groups.

"Gingerbread figures in the shape of Jim Crow, and other popularities

In the old burial-ground, Charter St. a slate grave-stone, carved round the borders, to the memory of "Col. John Hathorne, Esq." who died in 1717. This was the witch-judge. The stone is sunk deep into the earth, and leans forward, and the grass grows very long around it; and what with the moss, it was rather difficult to make out the date &c. Other Hathornes lie buried in a range with him, on either side.

In a corner of the burial ground, close under Dr. Peabody's garden fence, are the most ancient stones remaining in the burial ground, — in moss-grown, deeply sunken. One to Dr. John Swinnerton, Physician — in 1688, I think — another to his wife. There too is the grave of Nathaniel Mather, the younger brother of Cotton, and inscribed in the illegible, as a hard Student and of great promise. "An aged man at nineteen years," saith the grave stone. It affected me considerably, when I had swept away the grass from the half-buried stones, and read their names. A pebble two or three hung over these old graves, and there

often betraying plebeianism by the tones of their voices— Two girls on the common very tired—one a pale, thin, languid looking creature; the other plump, rosy, rather over-burdened with her own little body. Conversation of the various groups.

Gingerbread figures in the shape of Jim Crow, and other popularities

In the old burial-ground, Charter St. a slate grave-stone, carved round the borders, to the memory of "Col. John Hathorne, Esq." who died in 1717. This was the witch-judge. The stone is sunk deep into the earth, and leans forward, and the grass grows very long around it; and what with the moss, it was rather difficult to make out the date &c. Other Hathornes lie buried in a range with him, on either side.

In a corner of the burial ground, close under Dr. Peabody's garden fence, are the most ancient stones remaining in the burial-ground;—moss-grown, deeply sunken. One to "Dr. John Swinnerton, Phisition"—in 1688, I think—another to his wife. There too is the grave of Nathanael Mather, the younger brother of Cotton, and mentioned in the Magnalia, as a hard student and of great promise. "An aged man at nineteen years," saith the grave stone; it affected me considerably, when I had away the grass from the half buried stone, and read the name. An apple-tree or two hang over these old graves, and throw

down its blighted fruit on Nathaniel
Hathorne from — he blighted too. It gives
queer ideas, to think how convenient to
Dr. Peabody's family, this burial-ground
is, the monument standing also out within arm's reach of the side windows of
the parlor, — and there being a little
gate from the back-yard, through which
we step forth upon these old graves aforesaid; and the tomb of the Pickman family
is right in front and close to the gate;
it is now filled with corpses, the last
being the old refugee Col. Pickman and his
wife; — and the family have been compelled to seek another place to bury their
dead. Mercy Peabody, for the sake of
favors done her by the Mrs. Pickman
last deceased, has trained flowers over
this tomb.

    It is not, I think, the most ancient
families that have tombs — their ancestors, for two or three generations, having
been deposited in the earth, before such
a luxury as a tomb was thought of. Men
who founded families and grew rich,
a century or so ago, were probably the
first. There is a tomb of the Lyndes,
with a slab of slate affixed to the
brick masonry, on one side, and carved
with a coat of arms

down the blighted fruit on Nathanael Mather's grave—he blighted too.
It gives queer ideas, to think how convenient to Dr. Peabody's family
this burial-ground is, the monuments standing almost within arm's
reach of the side windows of the parlor;—and there being a little gate
from the back-yard, through which we step forth upon those old
graves aforesaid; and the tomb of the Pickman family is right in front
and close to the gate; it is now filled with corpses, the last being the
old refugee Col. Pickman and his wife;—and the family have been
compelled to seek another place to bury their dead. Mary Peabody,
for the sake of favors done her by the Mrs. Pickman last deceased, has
trained flowers over this tomb.

It is not, I think, the most ancient families that have tombs—their
ancestors for two or three generations, having been reposited in the
earth, before such a luxury as a tomb was thought of. Men who
founded families and grew rich, a century or so ago, were probably
the first. There is a tomb of the Lyndes with a slab of slate affixed to
the brick masonry, on one side, and carved with a coat of arms.

July 10th. A fishing-excursion last tide, wading afternoon, eight or ten miles out in the harbor. A fine wind out, which died away towards evening, and finally became quite calm. We cooked our fish on a rock named "Saturn", about forty or more feet long and twenty broad, irregular in its surface, and of uneven surface, with pools of water, here and there, left by the tide.— dark brown rock, or whitish; there was the dung of sea-fowl scattered on it, and a few feathers. The water deep around the rock, and swelling up and down, waving the sea-weed. We built two fires, which, as the dusk deepened, cast a red gleam over the rock and the waves, and made the sea, on the side from the Marsh, look dismal; but by and bye up came the moon, red as a lobster afire, and as it rose, it grew silvery bright, and threw a line of silver across the calm sea. Beneath the moon and the horizon — the commencement of its track of brightness — there is a cone of blackness, or very black blue. It was after nine before we finished supper. while we ate by firelight and moonlight, and then went aboard our decked boat again — no safe achievement, in our ticklish little dory. So thus remaining in the boat, we had looked very picturesque around our fires, and on the rock above them — our statures being apparently increased, to the size of those of Saul. The tide ever coming up, gradually drew near over the fires we had left, and as the

July 10th.

A fishing excursion last Saturday afternoon, eight or ten miles out in the harbor. A fine wind out, which died away towards evening, and finally became quite calm. We cooked our fish on a rock name "Satan," about forty or more feet long and twenty broad, irregular in its shape, and of uneven surface, with pools of water, here and there, left by the tide—dark brown rock, or whitish; there was the dung of sea-fowl scattered on it, and a few feathers. The water deep around the rock, and swelling up and downward, waving the sea-weed. We built two fires, which, as the dusk deepened, cast a red gleam over the rock and the waves, and made the sea, on the side from the sunset, look dismal; but by and bye up came the moon, red as a house afire; and as it rose, it grew silvery bright, and threw a line of silver across the calm sea. Beneath the moon and the horizon—the commencement of its track of brightness—there is a cone of blackness, or very black blue. It was after nine before we finished supper, which we ate by firelight and moonshine; and then went aboard our decked-boat again—no safe achievement, in our ticklish little dory. To those remaining in the boat, we had looked very picturesque around our fires, and on the rock above them—our statures being apparently increased, to the size of sons of Anack. The tide now coming up, gradually dashed over the fires we had left, and so the rock again became a desert. The wind and now entirely died away, leaving the sea smooth as glass, except a quiet swell; and we could only float along as the tide bore us, almost imperceptibly. It was as beautiful a night as ever shone — calm, warm, bright, the moon being at full. On one side of us was Marblehead light-house — on the other Baker's Island; and both, by the influence of the moon light, had a silvery hue, unlike their ruddy beacon-tinge, in dark nights. They threw long reflections across the sea, like the moon. Thus we floated slowly still the tide till about midnight, and then, the tide turned off. We tied our vessel to a pole, which marked a rock, so as to prevent being carried back by the reflux. Some of the passengers turned in below; some stretched themselves on deck. Some walked about, smoking cigars. I kept the deck all night. Now there was a little cat's paw of a breeze, whereupon we untied ourselves from the pole; but the breeze almost immediately died away, and we were compelled to make fast again. About two o'clock uprose the morning-star, a round, red fiery ball, very comparable to the moon at its rising — and getting upward, it shone marvellously bright, and threw its long reflection into the sea, like the moon, and the two light-rock again became a desert. The wind had now entirely died away, leaving the sea smooth as glass, except a quiet swell; and we could only float along as the tide bore us, almost imperceptibly. It was as beautiful a night as ever shone—calm, warm, bright, the moon being at full. On one side of us was Marblehead light-house—on the other Baker's Island; and both, by the influence of the moon light, had a silvery hue, unlike their ruddy beacon-tinge, in dark nights. They threw long reflections across the sea, like the moon. Thus we floated slowly with the tide till about midnight, and then, the tide turning, we tied our vessel to a pole, which marked a rock, so as to prevent being carried back by the reflux. Some of the passengers turned in below; some stretched themselves on deck; some walked about, smoking cigars. I kept the deck all night. Once there was a little cat's paw of a breeze, whereupon we untied ourselves from the pole; but the breeze almost immediately died away, and we were compelled to make fast again. About two °clock uprose the morning-star—a round, red fiery ball, very comparable to the moon at its rising—and getting upward, it shone marvellously bright, and threw its long reflection into the sea, like the moon and the two light-houses. It was Venus, and the brightest star I ever beheld; it was in the north-east. The moon made but a very small circuit in the sky, though it shone all night. The northern lights shot upward to the zenith, during the night. Between two and three o'clock, the first streak of dawn appeared, the daylight along the edge of the eastern horizon, a faint streak of light. Then it gradually broadened and deepened, and became a deep saffron tint, with violet above, and then an ethereal and transparent blue. The saffron became intermixed with splendor, kindling and brightening, Daheim? Planet light being in the center of the brightening, so that they were extinguished by it, or at least grew invisible. On the other side of the boat, the Marblehead light-house still threw out its silvery gleam, and the moon then brightly too; and its light looked very singular, mingling with the growing daylight. It was not like the moonshine brightening, as the evening twilight darkens; for now it threw its radiance over the landscape, the green and other tints of which were displayed by the daylight; whereas, at evening, all those tints are obscured. It looked like a milder sunshine — a dreamy sunshine, the sunshine of a world not quite so real and material as this. All night, we heard being the ship's clanging clocks telling the hour. Soon, up came the sun, without any bustle, but quietly,

houses. It was Venus, and the brightest star I ever beheld; it was in
the north-east. The moon made but a very small circuit in the sky;
though it shone all night. The northern lights shot upward to the
zenith, during the night. Between two and three °clock, the first streak
of dawn appeared, stretching far along the edge of the eastern
horizon; a faint streak of light; then it gradually broadened and
deepened; and became a deep saffron tint, with violet above, and then
an ethereal and transparent blue. The saffron became intermixed with
splendor, kindling and kindling, Baker's Island lights being in the
center of the brightness, so that they were extinguished by it, or at
least grew invisible. On the other side of the boat, the Marblehead
light-house still threw out its silvery gleam, and the moon shone
brightly too; and its light looked very singular, mingling with the
growing daylight. It was not like the moonshine brightening as the
evening twilight deepens; for now it threw its radiance over the
landscape, the green and other tints of which were displayed by the
day light; whereas, at evening, all those tints are obscured. It looked
like a milder sunshine—a dreamy sunshine, the sunshine of a world
not quite so real and material as this. All night, we had heard the
Marblehead clocks telling the hour. Anon, up came the sun, without
any bustle, but quietly,

his antecedent splendors having filled the sea, for some time previous. It had been cold towards morning, but now grew warm, and gradually becoming hot in the sun. A breeze sprang up, but our first use of it was to get aground on Coney island, about four oclock, when we lay till nine or thereabout, and then floated slowly up to the wharf. The scan of distant surf, through the night; the rolling of porpoises, the passing of shoals of fish; a seal seen. A steamer boat making along at a distance. I fished during the night; and feeling something pulling on the line, drew up with great eagerness and vigor. It was two of those broad-leaved sea-weeds, with stems like a snake, both rooted on a stone, which both came up together; often these sea-weeds root themselves on mussels. In the morning, our pilot killed a flounder with the boat-hook, the poor fish thinking himself secure on the bottom.

Cumberland, in the cuore of the heaven — on entering a distant celestial region, the fire in his heart and brain died away for a season, but was replenished again on returning to earth. So weary it be with me, in my projected three months seclusion from old aspirations.

Remembrance of a miser — to hug the drafts of his heart, in his tent

his antecedent splendors having gilded the sea, for some time
previous. It had been cold towards morning, but now grew warm, and
gradually burning hot in the sun. A breeze sprang up, but our first use
of it was to get aground on Coney island, about five °clock, where we
lay till nine or thereabouts, and then floated slowly up to the wharf.
The roar of distant surf, through the night; the rolling of porpoises,
the passing of shoals of fish, a seal seen. A steam boat smokes along at
a distance. I fished during the night; and feeling something on the
line, drew up with great eagerness and vigor. It was two of those
broad-leaved sea-weeds, with stems like a snake, both rooted on a
stone, all which came up together; often these sea-weeds root
themselves on muscles. In the morning, our pilot killed a flounder
with the boat-hook, the poor fish thinking himself secure on the
bottom.

Landerlad, in the Curse of Kehama—on visiting a certain celestial
region, the fire in his heart and brain died away for a season, but was
rekindled again on returning to earth. So may it be with me, in my
projected three month's seclusion from old associations.

Punishment of a miser—to pay the drafts of his heir, in his tomb

July 18th 1838. A show of wax figures, consisting almost wholly of murderers and their victims,— Gibbs and Wansley the Pirates; and the Dutch girl whom Gibbs kept and finally murdered. Gibbs and Wansley were admirably done, as natural as life; and many people, who had known Gibbs, would not, according to the showman, be convinced that this wax figure was not his skin stuffed. The two pirates were represented with halters round their necks, just ready to be turned off; and the Sheriff behind them with his watch, waiting for the moment. The clothes, halters, and Gibbs' hair, were authentic. E. K. Avery and Cornell,— the former a figure in black, leaning on the back of a chair; in the attitude of a clergyman about to pray,— an ugly devil, said to be a good likeness. Ellen Jewett and R. P. Robinson;— she draped richly in extreme fashion, and very pretty. He awkward and stiff, it being difficult to stuff a figure to look like a gentleman. The showman seemed very proud of Ellen Jewett, and spoke of her power as if this waxen figure were a real creature. Strang and Mrs. Whipple, who together murdered the husband of the latter. Lastly the Siamese twins. The showman is careful to call his exhibition the "Statuary;" he walks to and fro before the figures, talking of the history of the persons, the moral lessons to be drawn therefrom, and especially the excellence of the wax-work.

July 13th 1838.

A show of wax figures, consisting almost wholly of murderers and their victims;— Gibbs and Wansley the Pirates; and the Dutch girl whom Gibbs kept and finally murdered. Gibbs and Wansly were admirably done, as natural as life; and many people, who had known Gibbs, would not, according to the showman, be convinced that this wax figure was not his skin stuffed. The two pirates were represented with halters round their necks, just ready to be turned off; and the sheriff behind them with his watch, waiting for the moment. The clothes, halters, and Gibbs' hair, were authentic. E K. Avery and Cornell, the former a figure in black, leaning on the back of a chair, in the attitude of a clergyman about to pray;—an ugly devil, said to be a good likeness. Ellen Jewett and R. P. Robinson;—she dressed richly in extreme fashion, and very pretty; he awkward and stiff, it being difficult to stuff a figure to look like a gentleman. The showman seemed very proud of Ellen Jewett, and spoke of her somewhat as if this wax figure was a real creature. Strang and Mrs. Whipple, who together murdered the husband of the latter. Lastly the Siamese Twins. The showman is careful to call his exhibition the "Statuary"; he walks to and fro before the figures, talking of the history of the persons, the moral lessons to be drawn therefrom, and especially the excellence of the wax-work.

He has printed histories of the personages for sale. He is a friendly, easy-mannered sort of a half-genteel character, whose talk has been unfolded by the persons who most frequent such a show — an air of superiority of information, a moral instructor, imbued with a good deal of real knowledge of the world. Inviting his departing guests to call again and bring their friends. Desiring to know whether they are pleased. Telling that he had a thousand people the 6th of July, and that they were all perfectly satisfied. Talking with the female visitors, and remarking on Ellen Kwetts person and dress to them — he being "spared no expense in dressing her" and all the ladies say that a cheaper never sat beneath; and he thinks he never saw "a handsomer female." He goes to and fro, snuffing the candles, and now and then holding one close to the face of a favorite figure; ever and anon, hearing steps upon the staircase, he goes to admit a new visitor. The visitors, a half-bumpkin, half country-squire like man, who has something of a knowing air, and yet look and listen with a good deal of simplicity and faith, smiling between whiles; — a mechanic of the town; — several decent-looking girls and women, who eye Ellen herself with more interest than the other figures, all women having much curiosity about such ladies; — a gentleman only sort of boy.

He has printed histories of the personages for sale. He is a friendly, easy-mannered sort of a half-genteel character, whose talk has been moulded by the persons who most frequent such a show—an air of superiority of information, a moral instructor, mingled with a good deal of real knowledge of the world. Inviting his departing guests to call again and bring their friends. Desiring to know whether they are pleased. Telling that he had a thousand people the 4th of July, and that they were all perfectly satisfied. Talking with the female visitors, and remarking on Ellen Jewett's person and dress to them—he having "spared no expense in dressing her, and all the ladies say that a dress never sat better; and he thinks he never knew a "handsomer female." He goes to and fro, snuffing the candles, and now and then holding one close to the face of a favorite figure; ever and anon, hearing steps upon the staircase, he goes to admit a new visitor. The visitors, a half bumpkin, half country-squire like man, who has something of a knowing air, and yet look and listens with a good deal of simplicity and faith, smiling between whiles;— a mechanic of the town;— several decent-looking girls and women, who eye Ellen Jewett with more interest than the other figures, all women having much curiosity about such ladies;— a gentlemanly sort of per-

tor, who looks some what ashamed of himself for being there, and glances at one knowingly, as if to intimate that he was conscious of being out of place, a boy or two; and myself, who examine wax faces and flesh ones with equal interest. A political or other satire might be made, by describing a series of wax figures of the prominent public men; and by the remarks of the showman and the spectators, their characters and public standing might be exposed. And the incident of Judge Tyler, as related by E. P. P. might be introduced.

A series of strange, mysterious, dreadful events to occur, wholly destructive of a person's happiness. He to imbate them to various persons and causes, but ultimately finds out that he is himself the sole agent. Moral, that our welfare depends on ourselves.

The strange accident in the court of Charles IX of France — he and five other maskers being attired in coats of linen, covered with pitch and bestuck with flax, to represent hairy savages. They entered the hall dancing, the five being fastened together, and the king in front; by accident the five were set on fire with a torch. Two were burned to death on the spot, two afterwards died — one flung to the buttery, and plunged into a vessel of water. It might be related as the fate of a squad of dissolute men.

son, who looks somewhat ashamed of himself for being there, and glances at me knowingly, as if to intimate that he was conscious of being out of place; a boy or two; and myself, who examine wax faces and flesh ones with equal interest. A political or other satire might be made, by describing a show of wax figures of the prominent public men; and by the remarks of the showman and the spectators, their characters and public standing might be expressed. And the incident of Judge Tyler, as related by E.P.P. might be introduced.

A series of strange, mysterious, dreadful events to occur, wholly destructive of a person's happiness. He to impute them to various persons and causes, but ultimately finds out that he is himself the sole agent. Moral, that our welfare depends on ourselves.

The strange accident in the court of Charles IX of France—he and five other masquers being attired in coats of linen, covered with pitch and bestuck with flax, to represent hairy savages. They entered the hall dancing, the five being fastened together, and the king in front;—by accident the five were set on fire with a torch. Two were burned to death on the spot, two afterwards died—one fled to the buttery, and jumped into a vessel of water. It might be represented as the fate of a squad of dissolute men.

A perception, for a moment, of one's mental and moral self, as if it were another person—the observant faculty being separated, and looking intently at the qualities of the character. There is a surprise, when this happens—this getting out of one's self, and then the observer sees how queer a fellow he is.

[other book]

Oct. 25th 1838. View from a chamber of the Tremont of the opposite side of the street, on the other side of Beacon Street. At one of the lower windows, a female at work on a ?; at one above, a lady hemming a ruff or some such ladylike thing. She is pretty, young, last mentioned; for a little boy comes to her knees, and she pats his head and ??? ??? motherly. A note on colored paper is brought her, and she reads it and puts it in her bosom. At another window, at some depth within the apartment, a gentleman in a dressing-gown reading, and rocking in a rocking-chair. &c &c &c. A rainy day, and people passing with umbrellas disconsolately between the spectator and these various scenes of in-door occupation and comfort. Still this sketch might be filled, and worked up into something that way going on within the chamber where the spectator was situated.

At the moment that had been has been devising a certain joke — a smile.

The history of a small lake, from the first till it was drained.

A perception, for a moment, of one's mental and moral self, as if it were another person—the observant faculty being separated, and looking intently at the qualities of the character. There is a surprise, when this happens—this getting out of one's self, and then the observer sees how queer a fellow he is

[other book]

October 24th 1838. ["23rd" *changed to* "24th"]

View from a chamber of the Tremont of the brick edifice opposite, on the other side of Beacon street. At one of the lower windows, a female, at work on a shift; at one above, a lady hemming a ruff or some such ladylike thing. She is pretty, young, but married; for a little boy comes to her knees, and she pats his hair, and caresses him motherly. A note on colored paper is brought her; and she reads it and puts it in her bosom. At another window, at some depth within the apartment, a gentleman in a dressing-gown reading, and rocking in a rocking-chair, &c &c &c A rainy day, and people passing with umbrellas disconsolately between the spectator and these various scenes of indoor occupation and comfort. With this sketch might be mingled and worked up some story that was going on within the chamber where the spectator was situated.

All the dead that had ever been drowned in a certain lake—to arise.

The history of a small lake, from the flood, till it was drained.

An autumnal feature — boys had raked together the fallen leaves from the elms along the street, in one huge pile; and had made a hollow, nest-shaped, in that pile, in which three or four of them lay curled, like young birds.

———

A tombstone-maker, whom Mr. O'B. knew, used to cut cherubs on the tops of the tombstones, and had the art of carving the cherub's face in the likeness of the deceased.

———

A child of Rev. Ephraim Peabody's was threatened with total blindness. A week after the father had been informed of this, the child died; and in the meanwhile, his feelings had become so much the more interested in the child from its threatened blindness, that it seems a feeble burden to give it up. Had he not been aware of it till after the child's death, it would probably have been a consolation.

———

Being dissatisfied with the position of Ibrahim's foot, in her illustration of the Gentle Boy, Sophia said, "He would not sleep because Ibrahim kicked her."

——

Singular character of a gentleman (Henry H. jfferson, Esq.) living in retirement in Boston — esteemed as a man of the nicest honor, and his seclusion attributed to wounded feelings, on account of the failure of his firm in business. Yet it was discovered that this man had been the mover of intrigues, by which men in business had been ruined, and their property absorbed, none knew

An autumnal feature — boys had raked together the fallen leaves from the elms along the street, in one huge pile; and had made a hollow, nest-shaped, in this pile, in which three or four of them lay curled, like young birds.

———

A tombstone maker, whom Miss Pea-body knew, used to cut cherubs on the tops of the tombstones, and had the art of carving the cherub's face in the likeness of the de-ceased.

———

A child of Rev. Ephraim Peabody's was threatened with total blindness. A week af-ter the father had been informed of this, the child died; and in the meanwhile, his feelings had become so much the more interested in the child from its threatened blindness, that it seems infinitely harder to give it up. Had he not been aware of it till after the child's death, it would probably have been a con-solation.

———

Being dissatisfied with the position of Ib-rahim's foot, in her illustration of the Gentle Boy, Sophia said, "He could not sleep be-cause Ibrahim kicked her."

Singular character of a gentleman (Henry H. i-gin son, Esq.) living in retirement in Boston — es-teemed as a man of the nicest honor, and his se-clusion attributed to wounded feelings, on account of the failure of his firm in business. Yet it was discovered that this man had been the mover of intrigues, by which men in business had been ru-ined, and their property absorbed, none knew

A perception, for a moment, of one's mental and moral self, as if it were another person—the observant faculty being separated, and looking intently at the qualities of the character. There is a surprise, when this happens—this getting out of one's self, and then the observer sees how queer a fellow he is

[other book]

October 24th 1838. [*"23rd" changed to "24th"*]

View from a chamber of the Tremont of the brick edifice opposite, on the other side of Beacon street. At one of the lower windows, a female, at work on a shift; at one above, a lady hemming a ruff or some such ladylike thing. She is pretty, young, but married; for a little boy comes to her knees, and she pats his hair, and caresses him motherly. A note on colored paper is brought her; and she reads it and puts it in her bosom. At another window, at some depth within the apartment, a gentleman in a dressing-gown reading, and rocking in a rocking-chair, &c &c &c A rainy day, and people passing with umbrellas disconsolately between the spectator and these various scenes of indoor occupation and comfort. With this sketch might be mingled and worked up some story that was going on within the chamber where the spectator was situated.

All the dead that had ever been drowned in a certain lake—to arise.

The history of a small lake, from the flood, till it was drained.

An autumnal feature—boys had swept together the fallen leaves from the elms along the street, in one huge pile; and had made a hollow, nest-shaped, in this pile, in which three or four of them lay curled, like young birds.

A tomb-stone maker, whom Miss Burley knew, used to cut cherubs on the top of the tombstones, and had the art of carving the cherub's face in the likeness of the deceased.

A child of Rev. Ephraim Peabody's was threatened with total blindness. A week after the father had been informed of this, the child died; and in the meanwhile, his feelings had become so much the more interested in the child from its threatened blindness, that it was infinitely harder to give it up. Had he not been aware of it till after the child's death, it would probably have been a consolation.

Being dissatisfied with the position of Ilbrahim's foot, in her illustration of the Gentle Boy, Sophia said, "She could not sleep because Ilbrahim kicked her."

Singular character of a gentleman (Henry Higginson, Esq.) living in retirement in Boston;— esteemed as a man of the nicest honor, and his seclusion attributed to wounded feelings, on account of the failure of his firm in business. Yet it was discovered that this man had been the mover of intrigues, by which men in business had been ruined, and their property absorbed, none knew how, or by whom; love affairs had been broken off; and much other mischief done; and for years, he was not in the least suspected. He died suddenly, soon after suspicion fell upon him. Probably it was the love of management — of having an influence on affairs — that produced these phenomena.

Character of a man who, in himself and his external circumstances, shall be equally and totally false. His fortune resting on baseless credit — his patriotism assumed — his domestic affections, his honor and honesty, all a sham. His own misery in the midst of it — it making the whole universe, Heaven and earth alike, an unsubstantial mockery to him.

Dr. Johnson's Penance in Uttoxeter Market. A man who does penance in what might appear to lookers-on the most glorious and triumphal circumstance of his life. Each circumstance of the career of an apparently successful man to be a pain and torture to him, on account of some fundamental error in early life.

(A. P.— taking my likeness, I said that such changes would come over my face, that she would not know me when we met again in Heaven. "See if I don't!" said she, smiling. There was the most peculiar and beautiful humor in the point itself, ~~that can be imagined~~ and in her manner as, that can be imagined.

A person to catch fire-flies, and try to kindle his household fire with them. It would be symbolical of something.

how, or by whom; love affairs had been broken off, and much other mischief done; and for years, he was not in the least suspected. He died suddenly, soon after suspicion fell upon him. Probably it was the love of management—of having an influence on affairs—that produced these phenomena.

Character of a man who, in himself and his external circumstances, shall be equally and totally false. His fortune resting on baseless credit—his patriotism assumed—his domestic affections, his honor, and honesty, all a sham. His own misery in the midst of it—it making the whole universe, Heaven and Earth alike, an unsubstantial mockery to him.

Dr. Johnson's Penance in Uttoxeter Market. A man who does penance in what might appear to lookers-on the most glorious and triumphal circumstance of his life. Each circumstance of the career of an apparently successful man to be a penance and torture to him, on account of some fundamental error in early life.

S.A.P.—taking my likeness, I said that such changes would come over my face, that she would not know me when we met again in Heaven. "See if I dont!" said she, smiling. There was the most peculiar and beautiful humor in the point itself, ~~that can be imagined~~ and in her manner, that can be imagined.

A person to catch fire-flies, and try to kindle his household fire with them. It would be symbolical of something.

Thanksgiving at the Worcester Lunatic Asylum. At noon and dance of the inmates, in the evening — a furious lunatic dancing with the Principal's wife. Thanksgiving in an alms-House might make a better sketch.

— — —

The house on the eastern corner of North & ∉ streets (supposed to have been built about 1740) had, say sixty years later, a brick tenement erected, wherein one of the ancestors of the present occupants used to practise alchemy. He was the operative; a scientific person in Boston the director. There have been other Alchemysts of old in this town — one who kept his fire burning seven weeks, and then lost the elixir by letting it go out.

An ancient wine-glass (Miss Ingersoll's) long stalked, small, cup-like bowl, round which is wreathed a branch of grape-vine with a rich cluster of grapes, and leaves spread out. There is also some kind of a bird, flying. The whole is excellently cut or engraved.

In the Duke of Buckingham's comedy—"the Chances"— Don Frederick says of Don Whd, (two noble Spanish gentlemen) —"Our Bed contains us as ever."

A person, while awake and in the business of life, to think highly of another and place perfect confidence in him; but to be troubled with dreams, in which this seeming friend appears to act the part of a most deadly enemy. Finally it is discovered that the dream-character is the true one. The explanation would be — the Soul's instinctive perception.

Decr 12th. 1838.   Do. 29th

Thanksgiving at the Worcester Lunatic Asylum. A ball and dance of the inmates, in the evening—a furious lunatic dancing with the Principal's wife. Thanksgiving in an Alm's House might make a better sketch.

The house on the eastern corner of North & Essex streets (supposed to have been built about 1640) had, say sixty years later, a brick turret erected, wherein one of the ancestors of the present occupants used to practice alchemy. He was the operative; a scientific person in Boston the director. There have been other Alchemysts of old in this town—one who kept his fire burning seven weeks, and then lost the elixir by letting it go out.

An ancient wine-glass (Miss Ingersoll's) long stalked, small, cup-like bowl, round which is wreathed a branch of grape-vine, with a rich cluster of grapes, and leaves spread out. There is also some kind of a bird, flying. The whole is excellently cut or engraved.

In the Duke of Buckinghams comedy—"The Chances"—Don Frederick says of Don John, (two noble Spanish gentlemen)—"One Bed contains us ever."

A person, while awake and in the business of life, to think highly of another and place perfect confidence in him; but to be troubled with dreams, in which this seeming friend appears to act the part of a most deadly enemy. Finally it is discovered that the dream-character is the true one. The explanation would be—the soul's instinctive perception.

Pandora's Box — for a Child's Story.

Moonlight in half-tints: — Sunset, and sun-light generally, Paintings.

~~~

A person to look back on a long life ill-spent, and to picture forth a beautiful life, which he would live, if he could be permitted to begin his life over again. Finally, to discover that he had only been dreaming of old age — that he was really young — and could live such a life as he had pictured.

P. H. Peabody.

~~~~~~~

A newspaper purporting to be published in a family, and satirizing the political and general world, by advertisements, remarks on domestic affairs &c. Advertisement of a Lady's lost thimble &c.

~~~

Lydia Haven — she was unwilling to die, because she had no friends to meet her in the other world. Her little son Foster being very sick; on his recovery she confessed a feeling of disappointment, having supposed that he would have gone before, and welcomed her into Heaven.

~~~~~

Rev. H. L. Connolly heard, 1755, from a French Canadian a story of a young couple in Acadie. On their wedding day, all the males of the Province were summoned to assemble in the Church to hear a proclamation. When assembled, they were all seized, and shipped off to be distributed through New-England — among them the new bridegroom. His bride set off in search of him — wandered about New-England all her life, and at last, when she was an old woman,

Pandora's Box—for a child's story.

Moonlight is Sculpture:— Sunset, and sunlight generally, Painting.

A person to look back on a long life illspent, and to picture forth a beautiful life, which he would live, if he could be permitted to begin his life over again. Finally, to discover that he had only been dreaming of old age—that he was really young—and could live such a life as he had pictured.

S. A. Peabody.

A newspaper purporting to be published in a family, and satirizing the political and general world, by advertisements, remarks on domestic affairs &c. Advertisement of a lady's lost thimble &c

Lydia Haven—she was unwilling to die, because she had no friends to meet her in the other world. Her little son Foster being very sick; on his recovery she confessed a feeling of disappointment, having supposed that he would have gone before, and welcomed her into Heaven.

Rev. H. L. Connolly heard /1755/ from a French Canadian a story of a young couple in Acadie. On their marriage day, all the males of the Province were summoned to assemble in the Church to hear a proclamation. When assembled, they were all seized, and shipped off to be distributed through New-England—among them the new bridegroom. His bride set off in search of him, wandered about New-England all her lifetime—and at last, when she was an old woman, the found her Bridegroom on his death-bed. The shock was so great, that it killed her likewise. —

" In the midst of the beauty of Nature, how it touches the soul to feel that it is superfluous to all natural necessity. It seems as if, when God had made everything in wisdom and benevolence, he added one touch more out of an ineffable love.

The caress of affection is superfluous, and therefore seems a touch of the Divine. It is in human affection what the last touch of God is in Nature." E. P. P.

{ JANUARY FOURTH 1839 }

When scattered clouds are resting on the bosoms of hills, it seems as if you might climb into the heavenly region — earth being so intermixed with sky, and gradually transformed into it. —

A strange dying, in burial, and after many years, two strangers come in search of his grave, and open it.

The queer sensations of a person who feels himself an object of intense interest and close observation, and various constructions of all his actions, by another person.

Little Foster Haven used to look into E. P. P's mouth, to see where the smile came from.

" There is no Measure for Measure in my affections. If the earth fails me in love, I can die and go to GOD."
E. A. P.

she found her bridegroom on his death-bed. The shock was so great, that it killed her likewise.

"In the midst of the beauty of Nature, how it touches the soul to feel that it is superfluous to all natural necessity. It seems as if, when God had made everything in wisdom and benevolence, he added one touch more out of an ineffable love.

The caress of affection is superfluous, and therefore seems a touch of the Divine. It is in human affection what the last touch of God is in Nature."   E. P. P.

JANUARY FOURTH 1839

When scattered clouds are resting on the bosoms of hills, it seems as if you might climb into the heavenly region,—earth being so intermixed with sky, and gradually transformed into it.

A stranger dying, is buried, and after many years, two strangers come in search of his grave, and open it.

The queer sensation of a person who feels himself an object of intense interest and close observation, and various construction of all his actions, by another person.

Little Foster Haven used to look into E.P.P.'s mouth, to see where the smile came from.

"There is no Measure for Measure in my affections. If the Earth fails me in love, I can die and go to GOD."

S. A. P.

Letters in the shape of figures of men &c. At a distance the words composed by the letters were alone distinguishable. Close at hand, the figures alone were seen, and not distinguished as letters. Thus things may have a positive, a relative, and a composite meaning, when seen at the proper distance. &c.

———

Selfishness is one of the qualities most apt to inspire love. This might be thought out at great length.

Sophia says, that passing along the street, all muddy with puddles, the sudden view the sky reflected in those puddles is such a way as quite to conceal the foulness of the street.

A young man in search of happiness — to be personified by a figure whom he expects to meet in a crowd, and to recognize by certain signs. All these signs are given by a figure in various garbs and attitudes, but he does not recognize that this the sought-for person, till too late.

If cities were built by the sound of music, then some edifices would appear to be constructed by grave, solemn tones — others to have danced forth to light, fantastic airs.

Letters in the shape of figures of men &c. At a distance the words composed by the letters were alone distinguishable. Close at hand, the figures alone were seen, and not distinguished as letters. Thus things may have a positive, a relative, and a composite meaning, when seen at the proper distance &.

Selfishness is one of the qualities most apt to inspire love. This might be thought out at great length.

Sophia says, that passing along the street, all muddy with puddles, she suddenly saw the sky reflected in those puddles in such a way as quite to conceal the foulness of the street.

A young man in search of happiness—to be personified by a figure whom he expects to meet in a crowd, and to recognize by certain signs. All these signs are given by a figure in various garbs and actions, but he does not recognize that this the sought-for person, till too late.

If cities were built by the sound of music, then some edifices would appear to be constructed by grave, solemn tones—others to have danced forth to light, fantastic ones.

Familiar Spirit, according to Lilly, used to be worn in rings, watches, sword-hilts &c. Thumb-rings were set with jewels of extraordinary size.

In a witch-story, some victuals, or some oral instrument, to be introduced, warm with the fire of hell

A very fanciful person, when dead, to have his burial in a cloud.

———

"A story there passeth of an Indian king, that sent unto Alexander a fair woman, fed with aconites and other poisons, with this intent, either by converse or copulation complexionally to destroy him". Sr. Thomas Browne,

———

Dialogues of the unborn, like dialogues of the dead — or between two young children.

A moral symptom for a person, being rich, to lose his own hopes, and take the faculty movements, which were hidden deep in the healthful visage — perhaps a seeker might thus recognise the man he sought, after long intercourse with him on unworthy—

Familiar spirits, according to Lilly, used to be worn in rings, watches, sword-hilts &c. Thumb-rings were set with jewels of extraordinary size.

In a witch-story, some victuals, or some iron instrument, to be introduced, warm with the fire of hell.

A very fanciful person, when dead, to have his burial in a cloud.

"A story there passeth of an Indian King, that sent unto Alexander a fair woman, fed with aconites and other poisons, with this intent, either by converse or copulation complexionally to destroy him."

Sir Thomas Browne.

Dialogues of the unborn, like dialogues of the dead—or between two young children.

A mortal symptom for a person, being sick, to lose his own aspect, and take the family lineaments, which were hidden deep in the healthful-visage—perhaps a seeker might thus recognize the man he sought, after long intercourse with him unknowingly.

Some wanderers on Ararat to build a fire with the relics of the ark.

Two little boats of cork, with magnet in one and steel in the other.

To have ice in one's blood.

To make a story of all strange and impossible things — as the salamander, the Phoenix &c.

The semblance of a human face to be formed on the side of a mountain, or in the fracture of a small stone, by a lusus naturae. + The face is an object of curiosity for years or centuries, and by and bye, a boy is born, whose features gradually form the likeness of that portrait. At some critical juncture, the resemblance is found to be perfect. A prophecy may be connected

A person to be the death of his beloved, in trying to raise her to more than mortal perfection; yet this should be comfort to him, for having aimed so highly and holily.

A monster to be the offspring of love. — The love between two beautiful persons

Some wanderers on Ararat to build a fire with the relics of the ark.

Two little boats of cork, with magnet in one and steel in the other.

To have ice in one's blood.

To make a story of all strange and impossible things—as the salamander, the Phoenix &c.

The semblance of a human face to be formed on the side of a mountain, or in the fracture of a small stone, by a lusus naturae. The face is an object of curiosity for years or centuries; and by and bye, [*the manuscript shows clearly "by and bye," but with the "e" on the second "bye" crossed out*] a boy is born, whose features gradually assume the aspect of that portrait. At some critical juncture, the resemblance is found to be perfect. A prophecy may be connected

A person to be the death of his beloved, in trying to raise her to more than mortal perfection; yet this should be comfort to him, for having aimed so highly and holily.

A monster to be the offspring of loveless love between two beautiful persons